BIO BARON

THE WAY IT WAS
Growing up in Wartime Holland

The Way it Was

Published by:
Exxel Publishing Company
323 Telegraph Rd.
Bellingham, WA 98226
Tel.: 360–671–2275

Second Printing
Copyright 2007 by Sid Baron

ISBN-10: 0-9785582-0-0
ISBN-13: 978-0-9785582-0-8

Online ordering information:
Visit www.sidbaron.com
sietze@msn.com

Mail your order for The Way it Was to:
Exxel Publishing Company
323 Telegraph Rd.
Bellingham, WA 98226
Enclose $14.95 plus $2.50 for shipping and handling (check or money order) for each copy ordered. Your order will be processed within 24 hours and mailed postage paid.

Or call Exxel Publishing to order a copy at: 360–671–2275
Your order will be shipped promptly together with invoice for $14.95 per copy plus $2.50 for shipping and handling.

THE WAY IT WAS
Growing up in Wartime Holland

SID BARON

TABLE OF CONTENTS

PART II

 # ACKNOWLEDGMENTS

The Way It Was started four years ago in the form of chapters in the monthly *Meadow Lark* publication. I want to thank all the readers of *Life in Opende* who frequently told me how much they looked forward to the next month's chapter. During the four years I spent on this project, there have been many occasions when my mind was in Opende while my beloved wife was talking to me. I blamed my hearing aid, but she knew better. Thank you, Margaret, for your kind patience.

My sincere appreciation also to family members in Holland, who read a few sample chapters. Thank you, Berend and Lida Boersma, Klaas and Anna Prins, Jilt Prins, Siette Vriesema, and all the members of the Tolsma family who grew up in the same house I did. There are many others whose encouragement was much appreciated.

Finally, I want to express my appreciation to my brother, Henry J. Baron. Throughout the past four years, we've cherished our time spent talking about and comparing memories from the years of our youth. Even though he is four years younger, occasionally memories of certain wartime events which were hazy for me were lodged more vividly in his mind. The hours we spent walking along the memory lanes of our youth were most enjoyable. His career led him from a PhD in English literature to a long–term tenure as professor at Calvin College. His encouragement and praise have motivated me to continue. For that, and for the many hours he spent proofreading and weeding out the errors in this manuscript, I extend my heartfelt thanks.

 **INTRODUCTION**

Writing and tracing the journey of my youth has been an extraordinary experience. As I called upon the hippocampus of my brain to bring alive memories from long ago, I mentally placed myself into the nooks and crannies of my youth. I focused on the people I once knew until their faces and voices became clear again. I began to realize that those who once touched my life in some way left an imprint that continues to enrich my life.

During my journey, I have also reflected on the impact that parents have on the life and development of a child. Training, conditioning, environment, role models, experiences, and genetics all play a part in making us who we are. Which is most influential in the life of a youngster? I have no conclusive answer. However, having been blessed with loving, God–fearing parents, a brother, and three sisters, as a child I came to value deeply the influence of a family's love and loyalty, as well as the resourcefulness and independence my parents showed during the Depression and war years. Perhaps you will be able to draw further conclusions as you continue to meet the people and the events that shaped my life.

At various times, when pressures, fears, and responsibilities weighed especially heavily, I have reminisced about the carefree first ten years of my life and longed to be back there, just for a little while. I remember blowing the petals from aging dandelion blooms and counting the remaining petals after a mighty puff, wondering if it were true that the remaining ones represented the number of children I would have. I remember searching for a rare five–leaf clover as I dreamed about my future. I remember watching birds busily building their nests and patiently hatching their young. These memories are merely nostalgic and romanticized dreams of what is now forever in the past and beyond the reach of grown–ups. In the imagination, however, they become very real once again.

My idyllic childhood changed as the war descended on our peaceful town in northern Holland. World War II had a profound impact on me and on the way I live and view the world. I developed a clear awareness of the fragility and preciousness of life. Another feeling that grew inside me during that time, and which still pervades me, was an enormous sense of gratitude for those who gave their lives so that I might pursue a wonderful life, with a family and children. I owe a debt of gratitude toward all who fought in the war, and I never fail to express that when I encounter someone who helped bring victory to the Allies.

My experience of the war also inculcated in me a strong sense of responsibility toward my fellow human beings, a principle my parents took very seriously during the war years and beyond. The anxieties, fears, and dangers of the war, as well as the faith and courage of my family, all prompted me to begin writing *The Way It Was*.

I invite you to enjoy with me the journey of my youth and the first eighteen years of my life in the Netherlands.

Sid Baron

OPENDE, NETHERLANDS 1944

It was early afternoon when our quiet classroom suddenly erupted with the piercing sounds of air raid sirens. Everyone bolted upright in their seats. Even as the teacher shouted for us to crawl under our desks for cover, we heard the eerie whistling sound of bombs screaming earthward. All around us was the cacophony of roaring airplane engines, exploding bombs, and the rattle of heavy–caliber machine guns. Through it all came the ear–piercing wail of the sirens.

Although I was terrified, at the same time I was curious to see what was happening. On all fours, I crawled over the hardwood floor through the exit and into the schoolyard.

The sky was filled with aircraft. German fighter planes were attacking hundreds of four–engine bombers on the way to the German heartland. The defense by Allied fighter planes was fast and furious. One moment they were corkscrewing upwards, and another moment they were diving. Sometimes one of the planes would go into a steep dive and then rise straight up, trying to get a tactical advantage on another aircraft. The success of the maneuver depended a great deal on the skill of the fighter pilot.

I lay on my back against the wall of the school building, watching the action with fear and awe. I was fascinated with airplanes and had studied the different types of planes used in the war. Now I saw that a Messerschmitt was desperately trying to outmaneuver a pursuing P–38, with guns spewing hundreds of .50–caliber bullets together with 20 mm. shells from its wing canon. The Messerschmitt was in a near–vertical dive, blazing away with all four machine guns. It looked as if both aircraft might slam into the school in another second or two.

Heavy–caliber machine gun bullets kicked up gravel in the schoolyard not far from me. A huge bomber corkscrewed toward earth in a screaming death dive, crew members tumbling out of the fatally stricken craft. Not all of the parachutes opened. I jumped involuntarily as one uniformed body slammed into pastureland adjoining the school grounds.

The Messerschmitt made one final, desperate effort to climb steeply away from the devastating firepower of the P–38. A moment later, it exploded into a fireball and crashed straight down.

PART 1

 EARLY MEMORIES

Children are rarely able to recall their first conscious experiences. Most of us spend our early years with reasonably predictable routines, creating no particularly lasting memories. Growing up in the 1930's on a farm in northern Holland, I enjoyed a rather uneventful childhood.

Ten years of my life would

Baron family just before emigration in 1948
(inset in front of family home)

pass before something occurred that was so unforgettable, so unpredictable and frightening, that it left a truly indelible impression on my young mind. The arrival of World War II in the Netherlands transformed my tranquil childhood into a series of vivid scenes and experiences never to be forgotten—a new world of bullets, bombs, and dangerous secrets, as well as acts of unmatched kindness and bravery.

Before the German invasion of the Netherlands in 1940, the pages of my memory are mostly blank—or rather, a kaleidoscope of hazy mental images. Still, after so many years, here and there a few clear memories emerge.

The Way It Was

Our earliest memories typically involve unusual or traumatic events, such as what happened in my life at the age of three. Dad's mother had been living in our house since her husband died almost ten years earlier, long before I was born. Grietje–beppe, as we knew her, lived in a small, private section of our house that had been added to accommodate her after Grandpa Sietze passed away. Every morning, Beppe came into our living room and sat in her favorite rocking chair. When I appeared, she opened her arms invitingly, and I raced for a cozy embrace and rocked in her lap. That fond memory might never have become permanently lodged in my mind except for one final, dramatic event involving Grandma Grietje–beppe.

It was spring of 1933 and close to my third birthday. Beppe was eighty years old. One morning, my five–year–old sister Betty found our beloved Beppe on the ground under one of the apple trees behind our house, where she had collapsed while hanging her clothes on the line. Betty stopped in her tracks; something looked terribly wrong. She called out, "Beppe!" but there was no response. In full alarm now, she raced for the house and burst through the door, yelling, "Mem, Mem, something's wrong with Beppe!" Mom followed her little daughter out of the house and found the lifeless body of her mother–in–law.

I was too young to comprehend mortality or understand what had really happened, except that my beloved Beppe had gone to heaven and would never come back. The flurry of frantic activity that followed, and the pain, tears, and sadness of my parents and other family members, all made a lasting impression on me even at that age. Grandma's death would forever remain my first conscious memory.

I came into the world in May of 1930, right in the middle of the dark years of a worldwide depression. Hunger, unemployment, poverty, and deprivation were everywhere, even in the little town of Opende in the northern province of Groningen, Holland. Of course, I was too young to know or experience any part of the depression. But early in childhood, I picked up adult conversation about the economic problems of the times.

Like many of the townspeople, my family lived on a small farm of about twenty acres, most of it pasture. Our brick house had a tile roof, unlike the thatched roofs of our neighbors. We milked cows and raised heifers, a few pigs, and a small coop full of chickens, as well as crops such as wheat, rye, hay, and barley. In the garden we raised all sorts of vegetables: potatoes, turnips, beets, corn, and, during the war years, some tobacco plants for Dad's pipe. In addition to the cow–stalls, the barn also stored a variety of feed and fertilizer that Dad sold to his customers.

Dad was an independent man with no appreciation for those who could work but preferred to accept government handouts. When my mother told me that Dad had started a small feed and fertilizer business rather than accepting government handouts, something about independence clicked. This principle would stick with me for the rest of my life. Even before my teenage years, I sold garden seeds in springtime to people in our neighborhood and in the Topweer area of Opende. Like my dad, I decided early on to be independent, never earning or depending on a regular employer's salary or paycheck to provide for my family.

Along with his skills in farming, Dad was musically talented, patriotic, stubborn, and well–versed in Christian Reformed theology. Membership in the Reformed Christian church, known to us as the *Gereformeerde* church, was a long tradition in our family. As far back as I can remember, Dad always served on the Christian school board or on the church council as either elder or deacon. He was dogmatic about theology but intelligent and knowledgeable. As an amateur theologian, he left a number of writings. Debating the finer points of his doctrinal positions and convictions remained one of his life–long passions. He was generally in agreement with the pastor, but if he was not, he let him know. He also enjoyed debating with certain clients as he went around selling his dairy feeds, fertilizer, and seed potatoes.

Dad was very busy with his farm, his business, and his service to church and school. He was an honest man, widely trusted and respected. For years he directed the band Crescendo, which continues today as a bicycle show band in the Netherlands, as well as in Europe and Japan. While visiting the land of our birth several years ago, my siblings and I were treated to a special, moving performance by Crescendo in honor of our now deceased father, who had founded and organized the band some seventy–five years earlier.

Meanwhile, my mother, or "Mem," as we called her, stayed busy keeping the family warm, nourished, and dressed. Despite her petite stature, she helped out extensively on the farm and in the fields, especially in the summertime, when hay had to be done and the weather was warm. She would rake, and in the spring when the cows were let out of the barn into the pastures, she would make the old cow barn spic–and–span for the summertime, when you could literally eat off the floor. It was a brick stone floor, but it was very, very clean.

On top of all this, Mom prepared a meal three times a day. Breakfast typically consisted of bread, while the big noon meal included boiled potatoes, some meats, gravy, and a vegetable such as beans, carrots, or potatoes with cabbage. After we had eaten, there was usually dessert, in the form of pudding made with wheat or rye and milk, with a little syrup added as a treat.

Mom was indeed a hospitable person. If a guest or an agent representing some dairy feed manufacturer came to the house, they were always offered a cup of coffee and a piece of cake or a couple of cookies. Mom was also strong–willed, patriotic, fearless, and conscientious. Only after being driven to exasperation would she bite my ear. Henry's small ears never did give her much to chew on.

She also had a sense of humor. I remember clearly the day someone from the town visited our house. He was invited in for a cup of coffee, a little piece of authentic Frisian cake, and congenial conversation.

While the visitor and Dad were deep in conversation, Mom pretended to be searching for something on the floor directly behind our visitor's chair. Using a small safety pin, she quickly attached a small red beet to the back of the man's coat without him noticing. I can still see her standing by the kitchen window with her blue eyes twinkling, laughing uproariously, as the man rode his bicycle down the sand path with a red beet swinging like a pendulum from the back of his coat.

Early Memories

Many people remember me for the often elaborate, sometimes mischievous, and always humorous tricks I've played on people over the years—a characteristic evidently inherited from my mother.

The rite of baptism in our *Gereformeerde* church was another strange, shocking event that would become a lasting memory. I was four years old when my brother Henry was born. On a Sunday about two weeks after his birth, Mom began fussing over the little guy. She explained that she was getting him ready to take him to church, where he would be baptized. She dressed him in a neat white baby boy outfit, which I had worn four years earlier when I was baptized.

Now I was curious. I didn't know what "baptism" was. What would they do to my little brother? Would it hurt? Would it make him cry?

"It won't hurt," Mom assured me, "but babies often cry even when nothing hurts."

In church, I sat in the wooden pew between my older sister Betty and my mother, who held my little brother. The church building was red brick, like all the other buildings in our town. To a four–year–old, the church seemed very big, although it didn't look nearly as cavernous when I attended a service there many years later. In the winter when it was cold, the janitor kept a large stove at the front of the church filled with coal, even during the service, to keep the congregation more or less warm. Instead of a piano or organ, our singing was accompanied by the local brass band Crescendo which my father founded. Of course, everyone was always dressed in their Sunday best.

This wasn't the first time my parents had taken me to church. The same man in a black suit always walked up the stairway to a small loft, where he would stand and talk endlessly. His voice projected loudly from his position above the congregation, long before sound equipment. Sometimes he seemed to get excited about something he was saying and would flail his arms or point his finger in every direction at no one in particular.

The Way It Was

All the grown–up people I could see seemed to hang on his every word with serious expressions on their faces. No one ever laughed. I could not understand what it was all about.

On this Sunday, Reverend Van Dyke would administer the sacrament of baptism to my little brother. When he looked over to where we were sitting, my parents stood up. He asked them a question, and my mother handed the baby to my father. Coming down from his perch in the loft, the reverend then reached into a pan of water and threw the contents on my little brother's head three times. All the while, he kept on talking. No wonder my brother started crying. Then the man climbed the stairs again, and my mother had to leave the church with the bawling baby. How cruel to wake a sleeping baby by throwing cold water on his little head! I wondered if that man had done the same thing to me four years earlier. Good thing I couldn't remember.

I also had a sister, Betty, who was two years older than me. My earliest memory of Betty involved a different kind of baptism.

The living quarters of our house were attached to the cow barn. One door and a hallway were all that separated our kitchen and living room from the space where the cows lived during fall, winter, and early spring. In the summertime the cows were in the pasture, and the barn was clean. Strange as it now seems, I have no recollection of smelling the contents of the gutter behind the cows while sitting at the kitchen table only a few feet away. However, I do remember smelling Betty one day.

Betty was playing behind the barn when it happened. My dad had hired an older cousin to empty the concrete pit of liquid manure and spread it on the field as fertilizer. The large wooden cover was removed from the pit, and the hired man proceeded to use a long–handled bucket to pitch the contents of the pit into his manure wagon. He must have seen the little girl playing not far away, but apparently he didn't see her fall into the pit. I don't know precisely how he managed to rescue her. He may have jumped in and grabbed her, or he may have fished her out with his manure bucket. Either way, he did rescue her. My sister still tends to pinch her nose when she thinks about her little swim in the liquid manure pit. She smelled bad enough to make a vulture faint.

Early Memories

Mom got her all cleaned up, and an hour later, Betty's clothes were hanging on the line. For a long time afterward, whenever she wore those clothes, I thought I could still smell cow crap.

Wintertime never passed without memorable moments, especially not in Opende during the late 1930's. One day, Dad came home with a red, swollen cheek and a nearly closed black eye. He had been visiting some clients and was peacefully bicycling along when some bully in Opende had hit him with a hard–packed snowball. The bully must have been hiding behind a hedge. Dad never saw him.

Another day, Mom came home with a mild concussion and a giant head-ache. She had gone ice skating on the Kaatspool. While she was standing still on ice skates, another skater didn't know how to apply the brakes and slammed into her. She fell backward, hitting her head on the ice.

Ice skating was a favorite and common winter activity. As youngsters, we all learned on the River Lauwers, the stream between our place and the neighbors. It also served as the border between the provinces of Groningen and Friesland. The river widened slightly toward our neighbors directly north of us, Lyckle–om (Uncle Lyckle) and Fintsje–muoi (Aunt Fintsje), Dad's sister. They had a large family. All our Boersma cousins were, without exception, outstanding ice skaters. Cousin Berend was close to my age, and I was jealous of his form, style, and speed.

Then the time came for my little brother to learn the art of ice skating. I can still visualize the scene. Little Henk leaned both hands heavily on an old wooden chair to keep from falling. At the same time, he needed to stay upright on the skates and work his legs in an effort to gain traction and push the chair forward on the slippery ice. Several times, the chair gained excessive forward motion, leaving the little guy no choice but to fall on his face. It was a painful process.

We didn't have fireworks, bottle rockets, or firecrackers, but New Year's Day was still the day to make noise. We just had to be inventive and devise our own noisemakers. All we needed was an empty paint can, a bag of carbide, and half a bottle of water, and . . . *kaboom*! The mixture of carbide with a little water would instantly produce an explosive vapor.

For the ultimate cannon, however, we needed a retired ten–gallon milk can. It would wake any sleeping man or beast for miles around. The bottom of the can was punctured with a hole just large enough to allow a lighted match to be pushed through. Then a small quantity of carbide powder was placed inside, and the lid was put on the can firmly. In preparation for the blast–off, the can would be placed horizontally on the ground and angled slightly upward by placing a piece of wood underneath it.

A few drops of water were then allowed to drip on the powdered carbide. It would fizzle and produce a highly explosive gas, which was ignited by dropping a match through the same hole used to add the water. The explosion was virtually immediate. The tightly secured lid would explode from the can with great force, often traveling three hundred feet or more. The noise was deafening, so we plugged our ears in advance. It was fun, exciting, and very dangerous. I was responsible for keeping an eye on my little brother. To walk in front of a paint can or milk can just as it was being ignited was dangerous.

I had once asked Mom about a certain man I had seen walking along the road. His head was tilted back and sideways, making it appear as if he was always looking over his left shoulder and scanning the sky. Mom explained that when he was a young teenager, he had been hit with the heavy lid of a ten–gallon milk can on New Year's Day. He had nearly died and would never get better than he was. After that, I firmly determined that I would be careful during the New Year noise–making celebrations, since I didn't want myself or my little brother to go through the rest of our lives looking over our shoulders, peering into the skies.

———————————

When springtime arrived, the cows were released from their winter stables and turned loose in the pasture. We enjoyed watching their unbridled excitement as the animals celebrated their new freedom of movement and the lush young grasses. They would grab quick bites of grass and then resume their running, jumping, pushing, and cavorting with all the other cows.

For little boys, sunshine, toys, and playmates spelled contentment. Toys were scarce in the early 1930's, and I didn't get a little brother until I was four years old. Yet I don't remember being discontented. It required just a little youthful creativity to discover that mixing water with sand produced the perfect raw material for building sandcastles, which became my favorite outdoor activity. We always had a small mound of white sand in our yard, which was used for a specific purpose besides building sandcastles. It was the custom that on Saturdays, the entire yard would be "groomed." This included raking the yard and sand path that led to our front door. As a finishing touch, Dad would spread white sand over the raked areas, making it all look well–maintained and neat—a reflection of the Dutch reputation for tidiness.

One day, while busy mixing a little water with white sand to build a sandcastle, I heard an unfamiliar sound. As it grew louder, I looked in the direction of the street near our house for clues. Automobile traffic was still very light in the 1930's. I didn't even see a horse–drawn farm wagon, let alone a car or truck that could be making the noise. Yet the noise I was hearing grew. Something was getting closer.

Suddenly, a huge, bird–like machine came screaming toward the house. Mother, concerned about my well–being, came flying outside and scooped me up in her arms as the machine roared overhead. But it was too late—I had already wet my pants. Whenever Mom heard the sound of an airplane, she came running for me. Unfortunately, she never made it in time.

Eventually I learned not to be afraid. However, in the future I would learn to fear the sound of airplanes for a whole new reason.

MERCHANTS, MILK PAILS, AND MONKEYS

In the 1930's, automotive traffic in our country was still very sparse. Horse–drawn wagons were common, but most people got around on bicycles. Some older people always walked, having never learned to ride a bicycle. In a farming community like Opende, even the merchants brought their wares to customers' homes on bicycles. This must have made shopping an interesting experience for housewives. I remember the clothing store owner arriving with one or two suitcases strapped to his bicycle. He would carry the suitcases into the house and display various items on the kitchen or living room table.

The general merchant came regularly twice a month. He was the most modern, because he literally brought his store to the customer's door on a horse–drawn wagon. He sold a wide variety of merchandise, including various grocery items, vegetables, some fruits, and candy. He was known as "Julian Banana," probably because bananas were an imported item in the Netherlands, and he was the only merchant in the area who sold them. Whenever Mom made a worthwhile purchase, Julian gave me a Chiclet–type square of chewing gum, which was a highlight for me. I made the chewing gum last for days. It might have lasted as long as two weeks, but I usually swallowed it inadvertently.

The most interesting means of transporting merchandise was the dog–assisted, three–wheeled bicycle cart. The dog was in a harness in front of the three–wheeler to help the merchant as he pedaled his heavy load along the highways and byways of the town. That was how Little Peter regularly delivered the fuel for our kerosene lamps. When prunes were in season, he would augment his kerosene sales income by selling the ripe fruit. In retrospect, it was a strange combination. Everyone in town knew the pleasant, diminutive Little Peter and his business of kerosene and prunes. At that time, there seemed to be nothing unusual about that.

One nice summer day, a catastrophic event occurred on one of Little Peter's routes. As he rounded a sharp corner along a sand path, one wheel hit a deep pothole. In the blink of an eye, Little Peter, the harnessed dog, the five–gallon cans of leaking kerosene, and two hundred prunes were all thrown into a heap. Little Peter and the dog were soaked in kerosene, and the prunes were literally floating in it. It was not a good day for this likable little man.

There were other memorable characters, such as Siebe Fodde, a junk dealer who bought and sold old clothing and rags. The Frisian word for that type of merchandise was *fodden*. Three–wheeled open wooden carts were very common in the days of my youth, and Siebe Fodde's mode of transportation was just like Little Peter's. Siebe would ride on the bicycle seat with his feet on the pedals, although he rarely pedaled. He was the chauffeur, and his dog, harnessed to the front of the cart, was the engine. Occasionally Siebe Fodde would come to our house to buy some old rags, and I remember him well.

On my way to school one cold, stormy fall day, I had raised my jacket above my head like a sail and was racing along at top speed with a howl-ing tailwind. Then it happened. About 200 meters ahead, Siebe Fodde, chauffeuring his dog cart, wheeled onto the road from a wind–sheltered driveway. He could barely see over the top of his heavy load of rags, but that wasn't really a problem; the dog always knew the way. Since Siebe had a full load, the dog knew they were on their way home. That was undoubtedly why the dog was pulling the contraption onto the paved road at full–speed from behind a tall, wind–sheltering hedge.

The full fury of the storm struck the cart as it made a left turn onto the paved road. As the cart began to tip, the dog lost its footing. Siebe toppled, and his rags went flying. They sailed everywhere. One oil–smudged piece of cotton headed straight for Juffrouw Jammer's stern face as she came biking into the wind. The rag wrapped itself none too neatly around her glasses and the bun of hair twisted tightly on top of her head. With her vision blocked, the town's most dignified lady panicked, squealing like a neutered piglet most indecorously, and headed straight for the hapless Siebe, whose misfortunes multiplied now as he found himself under her bike. The smeared face of Juffrouw Jammer on top of the grizzly countenance of Siebe Fodde remains a vivid memory.

But something happened shortly afterward which made the whole incident absolutely unforgettable. About a half–hour later, Dad came peddling by on his way home from seeing some of his business customers. He took note of the assortment of rags decorating bushes, gates, and tree limbs. He might have given the unusual sight no more thought, except that he spied one article that looked vaguely familiar: a pair of red flannel ladies' underpants, publicly showing off its wear and tear by swaying in Jan Wouda's apple tree. Dad stopped his bike to look more closely, and then he was sure. Later that day, at Mom's firm insistence, Dad snuck into Wouda's yard after dark, climbed over the fence of the apple orchard, hoisted himself carefully up into the tree, and removed the offending undergarment Siebe had collected from Mom only hours earlier.

This had not been a profitable day for Siebe.

When I was seven years old, sitting at the kitchen table and drawing on a piece of paper with a pencil was a favorite activity of mine, especially on rainy days. I could watch Mom busy herself with putting wood in the stove and preparing the evening meal, all the while smelling the delicious aroma of the meat she was cooking. I could stare out the window and watch the wind–chased rain come down and the low–hanging clouds flee away from the North Sea. I could lazily dream about all the things little boys dream about.

I especially liked to dream about the cute little girl named Ann in my first-grade class at school. The first day of school had opened up a whole new world for me: a room full of children, all my age. Ann was my favorite, with her black hair, brown eyes, and light tan skin. All the others had light-colored hair, blue eyes, and white skin, which would tan only during the summer months. I thought Ann was beautiful. She sat in the row of desks directly to my left. If I leaned over, I could have touched her, although of course I didn't.

Instead, one day I wrote on a little scrap of paper: *I like your nice black hair and brown eyes.* I printed the message in block letters so she could read it. When the teacher was looking the other way, I put the note on Ann's desk. I was thrilled when she gave me a little smile, and I daydreamed about her for hours afterward.

"What are you thinking about, Sietze?" Mom asked, rudely awakening me from my youthful romantic fantasies.

"Nothing," I mumbled.

Mom went outside to call Dad to come in for dinner. It was springtime and a very busy time of the year, especially on a small farm with a few cows, chickens, pigs, crops, and pasture land. Dad was always busy, especially with the clients who bought cow and chicken feed and fertilizer. Sometimes extra help was needed. Geert, Dad's regular full-time employee, seemed clumsy, quiet, and shy. He was probably not even thirty years old, but when I was seven, everyone over twenty looked old to me. I never poked fun at Geert; he was heavy and big-boned, and strong as an ox.

Every spring, Geert had to spread liquid manure on the field. The manure was stored in a concrete underground pit about eight feet deep, just outside the barn with the cow stalls and the gutter. The heavy wooden covers normally provided adequate protection against accidentally falling in, except when it was time to spread the manure and the covers were removed—as Betty had personally discovered a few years earlier.

To begin the task, Geert used a small bucket filled with oats to attract the horse. After putting the halter and harness on the horse, he hitched it to the open liquid manure wagon. He checked to make sure that the iron open-and-close valve, located at the rear bottom of the wagon, had not rusted shut over the winter months. After some mighty tugs on the handle, which was attached with a connecting rod, he was satisfied that the slide valve was operating smoothly. He hitched a small, two–wheeled, bladed centrifuge to the rear of the manure wagon. The blades would rotate when positioned directly underneath the open–and–close valve and only when the wagon was in motion.

Next, Geert had to fill the manure wagon. After removing the wooden covers over the pit, he used a small bucket attached to a long wooden handle to scoop the manure into the wagon. When the wagon was sufficiently full, he brought it out to the field and pulled the handle. The liquid manure flowed onto the rapidly rotating blades of the centrifuge, which flung the smelly stuff in every direction. Geert was out of harm's way, sitting up high in front of the wagon to guide the horse. Once the wagon was unloaded, he would return to the manure pit and repeat the process.

One day, Dad decided to check on Geert, who had been busy with the manure all morning. Dad found him bending over the tank, stirring the liquid poop with the long wooden handle. Geert didn't notice Dad, whose curiosity increased as he watched quietly a few feet outside of Geert's field of vision. Finally he walked to the edge of the concrete holding tank and asked, "Geert, what are you doing?"

Geert was surprised by his boss's sudden appearance. He tended to be nervous under the best of conditions. He took a quick look at Dad before returning his attention to stirring the manure with the long stick, which he had removed from the scoop. Then he started stammering, "Mm–m–my j–jacket fell in t–the t–t–t–tank."

"Forget it, Geert," said Dad. "You'll never want to wear that jacket again, anyway."

"M–m–maybe not," Geert replied, "b–b–but it's almost noon, and m–m–my sandwich is in my jacket p–p–p–pocket."

———————————

From comments my dad made from time to time, I could tell that, in his opinion, I would soon be old enough to help with the farm chores.

The Way It Was

He had ambitious plans for my time before school, after school, and on Saturdays. When I had reached the age of seven, Dad thought I was old enough to start learning how to milk a cow. I was already beginning to feel grown–up, and milking didn't seem like a difficult task. It was a sit–down job, and I had watched my dad milk his cows many times. He easily squeezed strong streams of milk from the cow into the bucket, which he kept clamped firmly between his knees. At times, he would proudly point to the foam on the milk immediately after finishing. I got the impression that the presence of foam on the milk was indisputable evidence of the superior skills of the milker. I decided that my filled buckets of milk would always be graced by a thick layer of foam.

The only thing that gave me some concern was the knowledge that the relationship between cow and milker was not invariably friendly. Even though Dad used a stout rope to tie the hind legs of the cow, it still allowed for some kicking room, especially if the cow was in a bad mood. Dad would then respond with some stern, loudly spoken words directed at the offending cow. Somehow, the cow seemed to understand that her milker was not pleased with any unwarranted movement of her hind legs.

One Friday evening after school, I sat down warily on the milk stool, ready for my first milking experience. I had insisted that Dad tie the hind legs very firmly. As the cow turned her head, I could tell that those large, normally trusting eyes were viewing me with great suspicion. Dad had given me a smaller bucket that I could comfortably squeeze between my knees. When the little bucket began filling up, I could stand and pour the contents into a nearby larger bucket.

I placed my small hands firmly around two of the four "handles" from which I would soon cause the milk to flow. I began to squeeze gently, not wanting to offend the large cow, which had already eyed me guardedly. No milk! Even after I began squeezing more aggressively, still no milk flowed into my bucket. This was humiliating, and when the cow looked at me again, I tried to think of some choice words I could yell at her. She had obviously closed her milk valves and wasn't going to give me the honor of milking her successfully.

Finally, I yelled something like, "Let fly, you stupid cow!" The cow turned her head to look at the little pipsqueak pinching her milk handles, but she seemed totally unsympathetic to my plight.

Dad had heard me, too, and came running. "What's the matter, Sietze?" Dad always called me "Sietze."

"The cow won't let her milk flow into the handles for me to squeeze it out. I only got two drops, and my hands are already tired of squeezing."

"Okay, Sietze, let me show you." He placed one of his big hands on the nearest milk handle and said, "Milking cows requires a special squeezing technique. Actually, it's more like a kneading action. Place your open hands on the handles, and then begin to close your hand, starting with the thumb and forefinger. That way you prevent the milk in the handle from escaping back up into the cow's milk bag. Then begin to close your hand tightly, one finger at a time."

He showed me in slow–motion. Even in slow–motion, he produced a strong stream of milk, which splashed noisily on the bottom of my small pail. Gradually increasing the speed of the action, he showed me the finer points of milking a cow.

"Okay, now try it again," he said.

Sure enough, the stream was feeble, but I did start getting some milk. Dad smiled and returned to his work.

Now I really put my shoulders—or rather, my hands—to the task. But after a few minutes, the milk I had coaxed from the handles barely covered the bottom of my pail—and there was definitely no foam on top. My hands were aching and tired. Although the cow didn't kick, she constantly shuffled her hind legs. Perhaps she was attempting to gradually loosen the rope restraining her legs. She probably felt like kicking the inexperienced little pipsqueak milker clear out of the barn.

After resting my hands for a minute, I resumed the task that had appeared to be so easy the many times I had watched Dad. With my forehead lightly resting against the cow's flank as I concentrated on my mission, I failed to notice that the cow's shuffling rear legs were getting dangerously close to the edge of the gutter, which was about twelve inches deep.

Then the cow's rear legs dropped down into the gutter, and catastrophe struck. The entire milk bag, complete with all four handles, was suddenly lodged in my milk pail. The soft underbelly of the cow pinned my knees down, preventing my escape.

With an alarmed voice, I yelled, "Heit! Heit! Ouch, ouch!" I always called my dad "Heit."

He came running, yelling, "What's wrong, Sietze?"

I couldn't respond because I was crying. Of course, Dad immediately saw my precarious predicament and proceeded to untie the cow's hind legs. As the cow stepped back onto the platform, my milk bucket remained lodged around the milk bag and handles. Dad removed it while trying to comfort me. My tears continued to flow, especially as I watched Dad pour the polluted contents of my pail into the gutter. I hoped I would never have to milk another cow.

I was relieved to know that tomorrow was Saturday.

The morning sun peered through slightly opened curtains, casting golden streaks across the floor in my bedroom. I slept in a large, completely enclosed bed, almost like a box, with a floor, ceiling, three walls, and double doors. Since the alcove was elevated about three feet above ground level, to get into my bed I had to climb on a chair, open the two outward–swinging doors, and climb in. I never closed the doors, because my bed–cubicle would become pitch dark.

I hadn't slept well the previous night. Now, as wakefulness fully returned, I could feel my aching hands. In restless dreams, I had been fighting with a cow all night, trying to get the milk from the cow's bag into my bucket. The stubborn cow had simply refused to release her milk into her handles, preventing me from squirting the milk into my bucket. I tried clenching my fists, but it was too painful. I knew it would be a long time before I was ready to milk again.

Suddenly I remembered that it was Saturday and I didn't have to go to school. I could play outside, look at my picture book, draw pictures, and dream about my first–grade sweetheart. Sometimes I would ride with Mom on the back of her bicycle to Surhuisterveen, located just across the Lauwers River in the province of Friesland. That was where Mom would go every Saturday afternoon to get groceries. With some gentle prodding, she would often buy a little bag of candy.

I opened the doors of my sleeping quarters wide and stepped onto the top of the chair. My clothes were exactly where I had left them last night. I pulled on my woolen socks, which came all the way up to my knees. From the other direction, my pant legs came down just far enough to leave my knees bare. Before pulling on my sweater, I needed to make sure that I wouldn't pull it on backwards. I had made that mistake several times and remembered the teasing I had received.

Mom was busy braiding sister Betty's hair. She stopped long enough to hand me a washcloth and said, "Sietze, go wash your hands and face with green soap." At least I was old enough to do it myself and no longer had to endure Mom's daily scrubbing.

When I returned to the kitchen, Mom had cut two slices of white bread off a large loaf, added a little butter and honey, and placed it in front of Betty, little brother Henry, and myself. Now we needed to wait for Dad to come in before we could eat breakfast.

Little brother Henry decided that the appearance of a slice of bread could be enhanced if he kneaded the whole slice into a ball. When Mom saw it, she yelled, "Hink"—she often called him by this nickname—"quit that! Look what a mess you made."

Henry placed his bread ball on his plate and examined his hands. Yes, they were messy and sticky, with breadcrumbs, honey, and butter lodged between every finger. Wanting to rectify the messy problem, he quickly wiped both hands along the front of his sweater. Now Mom really yelled: "Hindrik!"—she only called him "Hindrik" when she was angry—"You dirty little pig, look at your clean sweater now."

He looked at his sweater and, seemingly quite satisfied with his artwork, looked back at her with an expression on his face that said, *What are you getting so worked up about?* It was fortunate for him that he hadn't yet developed an adequate vocabulary to express himself verbally.

The Way It Was

After breakfast, I didn't have to help my dad with chores because of my aching "milker hands." I had exaggerated the pain in my hands quite dramatically and surmised that I probably wouldn't be able to milk, or do any kind of farm work, for that matter, for at least a year.

Well, at least it had worked today. I sat on my chair near the window with my animal picture book in my lap. I could spend hours reading about different animals and studying the pictures. Occasionally I looked out toward the paved road a few hundred feet in front of the house. I never wanted to miss a car or truck coming by. With little motor vehicle traffic on the roads during this time, any automobile made for an interesting sight.

Then something caught my attention. A man on his bicycle turned off the main road onto the sand path leading to our house. As he got closer, I noticed something very peculiar. Standing up to gain a better view, I realized that something was riding on the man's shoulder. I stared intently and couldn't believe my eyes.

"Mem," I yelled, "somebody is coming with a monkey on his shoulder!"

Mom quickly joined me by the window and exclaimed, "Oh my goodness, here comes Lange Hylke with his monkey." *Lange* meant "tall."

By now, the man with the monkey was in our yard, parking his bicycle against the side of the house. He opened the front door and yelled, "Anybody home?"

Mom took me by the hand and said, "Sietze, come along. You have to see this." More than a little curious, I didn't need any encouragement. I had never seen a live monkey, only pictures of them in my picture book.

"Mem, do monkeys bite?" I asked.

She couldn't answer, because we were now standing in front of this very tall man with a monkey on his shoulder. The monkey seemed to take in the scene, swiveling its head nervously and eyeing us suspiciously. When the monkey looked at me, I decided to play it safe, hiding partially behind Mom's skirt and clasping her hand tightly. I sure didn't want to get bitten by a monkey.

Lange Hylke made some small talk with Mom and asked her if I was scared. I'm sure he could tell that I didn't trust his monkey.

"This monkey is very friendly," he said to me with a smile. "He's never bitten or even slapped or scratched anyone. What's your name?"

"Sietze," I said shyly.

"Well, Sietze, if you give the monkey a little piece of banana, he will really love you." With that, he took a little piece of banana out of his bulging jacket pocket and handed it to me. "Just hold it up, and the monkey will come down and eat it right out of your hand."

Still suspicious, I took the little piece of banana in one hand, holding tightly to my mom with the other.

"Hold it up," commanded Lange Hylke.

As soon as I did, the monkey took a giant leap off the tall man's shoulder and stood right in front of me, with a begging expression on its face. My heart was racing as the monkey carefully took the piece of banana out of my hand. Holding the banana in its front paw, it jumped back onto Hylke's shoulder. After quickly eating the banana, it jumped down again and did a somersault right in front of us.

"That means he wants more," said Lange Hylke. He quickly handed me another piece.

I was beginning to like the monkey, so I held the piece of banana in my hand as an invitation. The monkey eyed me with satisfaction. It stood tall on its hind legs, rubbing its stomach in gleeful anticipation of another tasty morsel. This time, it ate the banana without jumping back on its master's shoulder. Immediately it went into the somersault routine again. Lange Hylke quickly handed me another small piece of dried banana. Again, the monkey stood tall while rubbing its stomach and looking at the fruit. It looked me squarely in the eyes and vigorously nodded its head, as if to say, "Is it okay for me to take it now?" I nodded my head in return.

Carefully the monkey took it out of my hand, eating it while standing upright. Then the monkey put its right hand on its stomach and took three bows. It was the ultimate expression of appreciation.

I was completely in awe and at ease now and had let go of Mom's hand. This was enormously entertaining. As I watched it jump back onto the tall man's shoulder, I secretly wished I could have a nice monkey like that. While Mom was talking to Lange Hylke and fidgeting with her coin purse,

I couldn't take my eyes off of that wonderfully talented creature. Then my eyes grew bigger.

No, this couldn't be! Yes, I was seeing it right. The monkey was relieving itself right on the man's shoulder. Lange Hylke didn't notice at first, probably because Mom was handing him a couple of coins. Then he yelled, "You damned monkey, you're pissing on my shoulder!"

Mom grabbed my hand again as we watched the dark wet spot on Lange Hylke's clothing grow larger. He quickly turned to leave, repeating in an angry voice, "Damned monkey . . . damned monkey . . ."

Mom and I stood by the window laughing as Lange Hylke mounted the bicycle with his damned monkey and pedaled down the path, the wet spot on his shoulder clearly visible.

When our laughter had subsided, Mom became serious. "Sietze," she said, "I want to explain some things to you. Let's sit at the table."

Mom was never formal like this. I knew she wanted to talk to me about something important.

"You know, Sietze, Lange Hylke is a poor man. He travels from town to town with his monkey, and people pay him a nickel, or sometimes a dime. It's really quite an honorable form of begging, because his monkey is entertaining. Lange Hylke is married, and his wife's name is Wobbelke. She's only about half the size of Hylke. They are poor people who live in the Juliana neighborhood. That's where most of the very poor people live.

"Lange Hylke, like many of his neighbors, often gets drunk, and that's why those people are always poor. But Lange Hylke doesn't steal like some others from his Juliana neighborhood. He tries to make his living with his monkey. That's much better than stealing. Maybe if Lange Hylke were a Christian, he would know that getting drunk and using bad words is wrong. Sietze, your dad has never been drunk. He doesn't say bad words, either . . . except for one time, when a cow made him very angry." She didn't elaborate. Squeezing my hand, she left to go back to her work.

I thought about all she had said, knowing she would want me to remember it for the rest of my life. One thought was disturbing. Mom said that the Juliana neighborhood people were mostly drinkers, thieves, and just plain poor folks who used a lot of bad words. My cute girlfriend at school lived in the Juliana neighborhood.

# THE MAGIC COIN

During the long, three–mile walk to and from school every day, I was often accompanied by my friend Kees. When the weather was good, we would walk home for lunch and then return to resume our classes in the afternoon. Kees always stood by the hedge in front of the house where he lived with his mother, waiting for me as I made my way to school.

Kees was short and heavy, and his head seemed too large for his body. He wore a specially designed wooden shoe because he had a clubfoot and one of his legs was slightly shorter than the other. The special shoe partially compensated for the difference, but he still limped noticeably. Several kids at school always teased and poked fun of him. I never did, because Mom had told me that Kees was handicapped and that I should always help other people, especially if they were handicapped. So Kees had become my friend. I had to cut my normal walking speed in half so that he could keep up with me, but I never let on that I slowed down for him. He didn't do too well in school, either, but he always worked hard at learning. I'm sure he always did the best he could. I knew it hurt him deeply to be teased by other kids.

Kees was especially scared of Teunis, who not only teased him viciously but threatened to hurt him almost daily. Teunis was the class bully; he was bigger than the other kids and always wanted to pick fights. Even though I was smaller than the bully, I told Kees that I would protect him and would figure out some way to make sure Teunis didn't threaten or tease him anymore.

Kees looked at me with his large, trusting blue eyes and asked, "How are you going to do that, Sietze?"

"I don't know yet, Kees, but Teunis isn't very bright, you know. I'll figure something out."

Teunis was not a good student and was always getting into trouble, even in the classroom. He must have been a constant aggravation to our teacher, Mr. Talstra. One afternoon in the classroom, Teunis started launching rubber bands at other kids. Mr. Talstra's gray crew-cut hair would have been rising were it not already standing straight up.

"Teunis, stop it right now," he commanded. But Teunis was having too much fun watching the surprised reactions from the targets of his rubber-band launching activities.

Mr. Talstra jerked his desk drawer open, and out came the feared ruler stick, a piece of wood about a foot long and one inch wide. Getting a few good whacks on the palm of an outstretched hand was no one's idea of a pleasant experience. The hand could smart for days. It was a penalty Mr. Talstra applied generously when, in his opinion, a student's behavior warranted it. With an angry, determined look on his face, he held the stick and commanded Teunis to come to the front of the class.

Teunis was very familiar with the stick and had no intention of voluntarily coming to the front. Now Mr. Talstra's face turned a deep, angry crimson. This certainly couldn't be good for our teacher's health. Mr. Talstra already seemed very old. His crew-cut was white, mixed with a few darker speckles. With long strides, he headed for the desk where the troublemaker was seated.

Teunis clearly had no plans to welcome the arrival of a furious teacher with a stick. Just as Mr. Talstra reached to grab him, Teunis scooted out of his seat and started running. With Mr. Talstra in hot pursuit, he completed at least three full circuits around the rows of desks, with Mr. Talstra yelling all the while, "Come here, you rascal! I'll get you yet."

The Magic Coin

The entire class watched the chase with a combination of awe, fear, and delight. We could all see that the aging teacher would not be able to catch the wiry troublemaker. Finally, breathing heavily, Mr. Talstra stopped at his desk, put the stick in the drawer, and started writing on his notepad. Teunis returned to his seat, always keeping a wary eye on the teacher's whereabouts.

After school, I saw Teunis being very mean to Kees. He kicked him in the rear and said, "Hey, you big fat–head lummox, you look like an accident your mother had." He may not have been so mean had I been right next to Kees. Nevertheless, I saw it and heard it. Kees did not react. The poor boy was accustomed to abuse.

I was furious and wanted to charge Teunis and beat the tar out of him. It took all the self–discipline I could muster to force myself to think before I acted. I realized that Teunis would meet force with force, and since he was bigger, I could easily lose a "tar–beating" contest.

Then I remembered reading in a little catalog about a precious silver coin look–alike.

"Hey, Teunis!" I yelled.

He turned to face me. His eyes were menacing, ready to respond to anyone who wanted to pick a fight with him.

In a calm voice, I said, "Teunis, I really want to talk to you for just a minute."

His eyes turned from menacing to curious, even though his fists remained clenched.

"Teunis," I said, "I know you like to tease Kees, and you know he's my friend. I'd like to make a deal with you." I could tell that his curiosity was piqued, even though he was still skeptical.

"What's the deal, Sietze?"

I stood a little closer and lowered my voice to a mere whisper. "I know where I can get a very valuable silver coin. If I got that and gave it to you, would you promise not to tease Kees anymore, but instead protect him from others teasing him?"

His eyes lit up. Teunis didn't even have a copper coin. With a silver coin, he'd be rich. "How soon are you going to give it to me, Sietze?" he asked.

"I think it'll take me about a week to ten days to get it. That gives you about a good week to practice being Kees's protector. If you goof up, you won't get the coin."

"Don't worry," said Teunis. "But if you don't give me the coin after ten days, I'll cut your ugly head off."

"Okay, Teunis, it's a deal." I didn't tell him that the beautiful fake silver coin was actually a trick coin that would probably give him more grief than pleasure. At least, that was what I hoped, because inside I was very angry with that bully.

I walked with Kees the rest of the way. He had been watching and wondered what Teunis and I had talked about.

"I'll tell you later," I said. "Right now, all I can tell you is that you won't need to worry about Teunis anymore."

He looked at me with those big blue eyes and said, "You mean Teunis won't be mean to me anymore?"

"That's right, Kees, and if he is, you let me know right away."

In disbelief, Kees stared at me for a few seconds and said, "Thanks, Sietze. I'm glad you're my friend."

———————————

When I got home after school, I told Mom all about big, mean Teunis, poor Kees, and the bargain I had made with the bully. She laughed when I explained that the beautiful coin was not only fake, but also a trick coin that would make Teunis smell worse than a barrel of rotting fish. Yet he would not be able to identify the coin as the source of the stench. Mom was convinced that it might work and gave me the money to order it. Then her face took on a serious expression.

"Sietze, do you know that Jantina van Dekken is very sick?"

I looked at Mom with surprise. "She sits right in front of me in the classroom," I said. "I noticed that she wasn't in school yesterday, and not today, either."

"Her dad stopped in today," Mom continued. "He asked that we pray for Jantina and said that Dr. Colett hadn't offered much hope that she would get better again."

"Will Jantina die?" I asked.

Mom looked at me with a somber expression on her face but didn't say anything. That was when I first began thinking seriously about death. After Beppe died suddenly, I had thought death only came to old people—not to the little girl with the dark blond braided hair, sitting at her school desk just ahead of mine.

Hours later, before going to sleep, I prayed that Jantina would be in school the next morning. That night, I dreamed about dying, frightening dreams about leaving the earth on a long journey to heaven and never being able to come back. Even when I awoke, I couldn't get the dreams out of my mind.

When I was still several hundred yards from school, I began looking at the activity on the playground. Maybe I could spot Jantina playing jump rope with her friends. When I didn't see her, I thought maybe she had stayed in the hall, where it was warmer. No, she wasn't in school.

When teacher Gorter came into the class, he looked very serious and sad. He didn't have to call the class to order. Everyone was quiet and looked at the teacher with some puzzlement, knowing that something was wrong.

Jantina VanDekken

"Boys and girls," he began, "you know that Jantina van Dekken has not been in class for a few days. She became very sick, and the doctor didn't know what it was. Early this morning, at five o'clock, she went to heaven. She's not with us anymore."

Never had there been such complete silence in the class. It seemed like all the kids were holding their collective breath, staring uncomprehendingly at the teacher.

After a brief pause, he continued: "During the three days of her illness, she remained cheerful. Even during the final hours of her life, surrounded by her parents, brother, and sisters, she smiled and comforted them by expressing her assurance that she was going to see Jesus soon and that a little later she would see her mom and dad, brother, and sisters again. Shortly before she died, she clasped hands with her family and began singing weakly, with her eyes closed: '*Ik zie een poort wijd open staan* (I see the gate of heaven opening wide).' Before she could finish, she peacefully slipped into eternity."

Our teacher swallowed hard, bowed his head, and was silent. Tears trickled down the cheeks of many. Some sobbed as young minds attempted to understand death. I think we all struggled with the baffling reality of that final departure. We didn't really want to accept that Jantina would never be with us again. His voice choking with emotion, the teacher prayed for the class and for Jantina's family and friends.

Three days later, I walked with my classmates behind the horse–drawn hearse carrying a small casket. Just ahead of us and closer to the wagon were Jantina's immediate family members: parents, siblings, uncles, aunts, and cousins, all in black jackets or overcoats. It was a dreary procession on a dreary day. Rain fell relentlessly from the heavens, as if nature protested the death of a sweet little girl whose life had barely begun.

The road was covered by a canopy of branches and leaves from the giant oak trees lining both sides of the street. We all walked silently, seemingly lost in thought. The cold raindrops falling on the oak leaves joined forces and cascaded in little streams onto the heads of those in the funeral procession, mingling with tears on the faces of those who had loved Jantina. The wagon creaked and trembled whenever the large, iron–rimmed wheels rattled through a rut in the road. I shuddered thinking about Jantina's body being jostled each time the wagon wheels hit a pothole.

It was still hard for me to fathom death. Those two long braids would never rest on the front of my classroom desk again. No more mock races or jump–rope contests on the school playground. Her life was over. She would never come back. Would she be able to see us from heaven? And if she could, how could she be happy, knowing that everyone in this somber procession was so sad? Wasn't everyone always happy in heaven?

I looked at her mother and father, two hard–working poor people. Now they seemed bent and broken, partially because of many years of hard work, but mostly because their little daughter would never again stretch her arms around their necks and say, "I love you, Mommy . . . I love you, Daddy."

When I saw that little casket carefully lowered into the grave, I cried too. It seemed so final. We were still in time, while she was in eternity. I didn't understand. I couldn't.

On my way to school, I saw Kees some distance away, walking by himself. Usually he waited for me by the hedge. He may have thought that I was late that day or wouldn't be in school. Slowly and laboriously, Kees plodded along, dragging his wooden–shoe–covered clubfoot along the hard–surfaced road.

I caught up with him quickly and draped my right arm over his shoulder as I drew alongside. He turned his head with a look of alarm, which quickly changed to a look of surprise and a friendly smile.

"Oh, Sietze, there you are!" he said as he looked at me with his large, friendly eyes reflecting good–natured kindness. "I waited for you but thought that you had already gone to school before I got to the hedge. I was a little late this morning."

"No, Kees, I'd probably still be waiting for you by the hedge if I hadn't seen you walking before I got to your house." He grinned and nodded his somewhat oversized head.

"Teunis has been leaving me alone lately," he said. "He doesn't even call me nasty names anymore. He's picking on other kids now—only those smaller than he is. I know I'm bigger, but he knows that I'm a cripple and I can't run."

"I'm getting worried, Kees," I said. "Every day he asks me when he's getting the silver coin I promised him. He reminds me every day that on Monday, the ten days are up. If he doesn't get that silver coin by Monday, he said I'm going to be real sorry. Kees, it's Friday today. If the mailman doesn't bring it today, my only chance of getting it would be tomorrow."

Kees looked at me with a worried expression. For a few minutes, we walked on silently. Then he turned his head my way and said, "Sietze, I know what I'm going to do. I'm going to talk to Tiete. He's your friend, and he's bigger than Teunis, and he's never been mean to me. I'll ask him to help you beat up on Teunis if he tries to hurt you on Monday."

Kees was right: Tiete was a friend. He was shy and self–conscious, and I had never seen him bother anyone. But he was one of the biggest kids in my class, and I was sure that he would come to my defense if necessary.

The following morning dawned bright and beautiful. It was Saturday, and I was busy raking the front yard when Mr. Dalmolen, the mailman, came pedaling down the sand path leading to our house. Draped across a baggage holder behind the seat were two large leather bags.

I leaned on my rake and watched him approach. Dismounting his bike with a flourish, he said, "Sietze, I have a very small package, and it has your name on it." Opening the flap of one of the leather mailbags, he extracted an envelope, the weekly newspaper, and a small package. "I see your mom is already by the door. I'll just give everything to her."

Dropping the rake on the ground, I quickly headed for the house, eager to see the coin I had promised Teunis. I was excited and relieved. No longer need I worry about getting beat up by mean Teunis on Monday.

Mom handed me the package, which I promptly but carefully opened. The coin was beautiful. I laid it on the table while reading the instruction sheet that was enclosed. Mom, who was also curious, read over my shoulder. She started laughing, and as soon as I caught up to where she had been reading, I laughed too.

Placing the coin in a warm area, or holding it in your hand for several minutes, will release a powerful and unpleasant odor through a tiny, nearly invisible opening in the center of the coin.

The Magic Coin

I looked forward to Monday with gleeful anticipation, certain that Teunis would clutch the coin tightly in the palm of his hand.

––––––––––––––––––––

It was a cool, cloudy, dark Monday morning, but at least it was dry. Walking along the sand path, it didn't take me long to reach the tree–lined street running from east to west through the little town of Opende. I spotted Kees some distance away, waiting for me by the hedge. The coin was safely tucked in my jacket pocket, where it would stay cool. As the instructions recommended, I had kept it in the little box, where it would not get warm enough to liquefy its secret smelly substance.

Looking again along the street ahead, I noticed that Kees wasn't alone. Tiete and Kees were waiting for me together. They would have served as my protectors in case I had not received the coin by today's deadline and mean Teunis beat up on me. Making sure the little box with the coin was in my pocket, I felt glad that I could make good on my promise to Teunis without coming to blows. I also gained a deeper appreciation for friends who were willing to come to my defense if necessary—especially Kees, with all his handicaps. I was sure that he could deliver a potent, painful kick to Teunis's shins with his heavy wooden shoe if given the chance. Tiete was a tall boy, quiet, and always peaceful. He was willing to come to my defense, even though I knew he would rather walk many miles to avoid conflict.

Teunis lived virtually across the street from Kees's house. He bounded out of his house and saw me coming a short distance away. Seeing Kees waiting for me would have seemed like nothing unusual. He may have wondered why Tiete was also waiting, but he decided to join them as I was approaching.

All weekend I had been developing a plan in my mind for how and when to give the coin to Teunis. I couldn't give him the coin in its pretty little box. It would never get warm enough to start melting its smelly interior. I still didn't have it figured out, and now, on this bright Monday morning, Teunis was waiting for me.

Teunis glared at me with owl-like eyes. When he lowered his upper lids halfway, he looked truly menacing. "Do you have my coin, Sietze?"

I didn't answer immediately. There was an uncomfortable silence. Kees tapped his clubfoot nervously on the pavement, while Tiete chewed his lower lip so vigorously that I feared he'd devour it at any moment. Teunis's eyes darted from one to the other. I was sure he was nervous, too. It was clear to him that I had arranged for a bodyguard, just in case the coin had not arrived by the promised date.

Glaring at me from beneath his lowered lids, he growled, "Sietze, do you have my coin, or don't you?"

"Teunis, don't get excited. I have your coin. It came on Saturday, and I have it in my pocket. Let's go to school, and before we go inside our class-room, I'll give it to you."

"Why can't I have it right now?"

My mind was still in overdrive, trying to work out the best plan. None of them knew why I couldn't give Teunis the coin right now. They couldn't know that I wouldn't want Teunis to have the coin in the little box. They didn't know that the coin was a cheap fake and that, given the right temperature, it would turn into a real stinker.

Taking the lead in our walk to school, I said, "Tell you what, Teunis—I'll show you this beautiful coin. After you see it, you will understand why I want to keep it as long as possible. Besides, you might have a hole in your pocket and could promptly lose it."

With that, I pulled the box from my pocket and popped up the small cover with a flourish, exposing the shiny, valuable-looking coin for all three to see.

They gasped when they saw the glittering coin. I'm sure they wondered how I could have ever promised Teunis such a valuable reward simply for doing the right thing and not mistreating poor handicapped Kees. The small cover clicked closed, and the box returned to my pocket.

"Sietze, I don't have a hole in my pocket," Teunis said. I was happy to hear that. "And I have never had a hole in my pocket big enough for that box to slide through."

Here was my chance. With my two bodyguard friends at my side, I boldly said, "Teunis, I've got some news for you. You may think that you're getting this coin as a reward for being a big, nasty bully. Not so. You are getting this coin as a reward for being nice to Kees the rest of your life. You got that?"

"Sure."

Emboldened now, I went on: "And Teunis, because I don't trust you too well, I'm going to keep the pretty little box. In case you ever hurt or are mean to our friend Kees again, we are going to wrestle the coin away from you with as many of our friends as it takes." Louder and bolder now, I almost yelled, "So, you big bully, I fully expect to get this coin back, and when I do, I want to have the pretty box to put it in!!" I exhaled, very satisfied with the plan that had come together so perfectly.

All Teunis could say was, "Fat chance of you getting the coin back."

As we entered the classroom, I slipped the coin from the box into Teunis's hand. He clasped it securely in the palm of his hand, which he then buried deep in his pocket.

Sliding into the seat at my desk, I could see Teunis sitting near the front of the class, three rows of desks to my left. We hadn't been in class more than ten minutes when I noticed some kids sniffing and casting suspicious glances at other students. A few moments later, I got my first whiff. I suppressed a chuckle and kept a serious expression on my face, knowing I was the only one in class who knew where the smell had originated and why. The smell was truly obnoxious, but it was difficult to pinpoint where it came from because it was so pervasive. It soon filled the classroom.

Mr. Posthumus, our teacher, had certainly smelled many whiffs before from gassy kids, but this was more than he could stomach. He quickly opened the classroom windows. Unfortunately, there was little breeze outside, and if a vulture had ventured in through the open window, the smell would still have been bad enough to make that vulture faint.

Mr. Posthumus left briefly and soon returned with the headmaster. Mr. Talstra took one step, one whiff . . . and quickly fled. We were dismissed for ten minutes to the school playground.

Fifteen minutes later, back in class, the whole smelly scene repeated itself. No doubt Teunis, completely unaware that he was causing a real stink, was clutching his coin again and warming it sufficiently to again release the smelly liquid.

The Way It Was

After the class returned to their desks for the second time, I whispered to Mr. Posthumus that I had been close to Teunis on the playground and could still smell it. After all the kids were seated again, the teacher went to the desk where Teunis was sitting, undoubtedly still clutching his unsuspected coin. Mr. Posthumus stooped to place his nose closer to Teunis's posterior, took a good sniff, and asked Teunis to step out into the hall.

I don't know what he said to Teunis, but he sent Teunis home and undoubtedly suggested that he take a good soak in a tub of water. I was sure Teunis would put the coin in a safe place at his house and that he would likely not find out about its secret. I couldn't be sure and would just have to wait until tomorrow.

Several hours after the smelly classroom episode, Kees, Tiete, and I were on our way home.

"Wha–wha–what do you think Teunis must have had for supper last night?" said Kees, who had a stuttering problem.

Tiete and I roared with laughter. I had never told them that the coin was the source of the odor. We continued walking and speculating hilariously about the various food items Teunis must have had on his dinner plate the previous night that had caused him to smell so bad today.

Tiete and I walked on after dropping Kees off at his house. Soon afterward, Tiete left along the sand path toward the place where he lived with his parents and one younger brother. The distance to my house was only half a mile now. As I walked, I continued chuckling to myself now and then about the events of the day.

Then the sound of an airplane reached my ears, and I looked up, searching the skies. This sound was different from the normally low–flying KLM airplane that I had seen nearly every day as it transported passengers from Schiphol to the Eelde airport in the province of Groningen. I didn't see an airplane, yet the sound was unmistakable. I needed to get away from the view–obstructing foliage of the big oak trees lining both sides of the street.

In the open now, I searched the blue skies above. There it was, looking no larger than a matchbox. I had never seen an airplane fly that high. What really alarmed me was the trail of white smoke coming from the airplane. Maybe it was on fire and the pilot couldn't see the smoke. Maybe it was going to explode at any time. I was eager to get to the safety of the house.

Then an even more fearsome thought struck me. I had heard my dad talking about the world war that had occurred between the years 1914 and 1918. He had been in the Dutch military service. Fortunately, Holland had avoided becoming involved in that war. I remembered overhearing stories of German airplanes releasing poisonous gas over the front lines of French soldiers. I had also heard talk of the likelihood of another world war, that Germany had already conquered Austria and was going after Poland, Belgium, France, and other European countries. Tiete's dad had mentioned that Holland could easily be attacked, even though it had declared its neutrality. He didn't trust the Germans under Adolph Hitler.

I looked up again. The swath of white smoke trailing the airplane became longer and wider. It was probably drifting toward the ground to poison us and kill us instantly. Fear banished from my mind all the earlier events of the day, and I started running. I needed to get home and warn my mother. Maybe the whole family could hide in the cellar.

I took a shortcut across a nearby field and noticed that Folkert Nobach was working on the piece of land he owned next to our house. I liked Mr. Nobach; he always talked to me like I was already grown up. He was short of stature and slightly stooped, with a friendly face. At the moment, he was so busy flinging pitchforks full of manure in every direction that he probably hadn't noticed the high-flying airplane releasing poisonous gas. He looked up and spotted me as I raced toward the house. He promptly stuck the teeth of the pitchfork into the ground and leaned on the tool. I didn't even want to slow down, let alone stop and talk.

I pointed at the sky above and yelled, "Airplane . . . throwing out poison gas . . . to kill us!"

Mr. Nobach glanced up and, to my surprise, started laughing. "Sietze, that's not poisonous gas. It's because the airplane is flying so high that the air is freezing cold. It's called a vapor trail and is totally harmless."

I stared at him, eyes and mouth wide open. He laughed again.

"Aw, Sietze, you poor boy. You were really scared, weren't you?"

A wave of relief surged through me, and I stammered something about thinking that Hitler wanted to kill us all.

Now Mr. Nobach took a few steps toward me and sat on his heels right in front of me. "No Sietze, Hitler is a good man," he said. "He would never do anything like that. This whole country would be better off if Hitler were the boss here."

I smiled and nodded agreeably before continuing the short walk to my house. *Wow*, I thought. Mr. Nobach's comments about Hitler were completely different from any conversation I had ever overheard between my parents and others.

I told my mom about the airplane with the poisonous gas. When she came outside to look, the airplane had disappeared, and the poison gas had transformed into small, wispy clouds high in the sky. I told her about my fear and my conversation with Mr. Nobach.

"Listen, Sietze," she said, indicating to me that she was getting ready to tell me something very important. "Folkert Nobach is a nice man, but in Opende he is known as an NSB–er. That means he is a member of Hitler's National Socialist *Beweging*, or Nazi movement. He would like to see Holland fall into the hands of the Germans. He would get power, and we would all lose our freedom."

I nodded solemnly in response.

An hour later, sitting on my milk stool with a pail between my knees, I pondered all the events of the day—especially my conversations with Mr. Nobach and my mother. I decided I would still be Mr. Nobach's friend . . . but I believed my mother, and I would never completely trust Mr. Nobach.

As I sat there in the green pasture, peacefully milking a cow on a beautiful spring day in May 1940, I could not have imagined how the serene world of a ten–year–old boy could completely change overnight.

PART II

WAR

A big hand on my shoulder shook me vigorously.

"Sietze, time to get up."

Dad's wake–up calls were never particularly gentle, but I knew better than to ignore them. I had learned that if he had to come back and call me for the second time, he would be ruthless. I was almost ten years old now and had to help milk cows every morning. Of course, I would have preferred to continue my slumber for a couple of hours rather than get up at six o'clock to milk cows.

It was early spring, and the cows were no longer in the warm barn. Milking was especially unpleasant when the weather was cold or rainy. This morning, Dad was either particularly impatient or a little cranky, or both—probably because the cows were out in the field, some distance from the house.

I dressed groggily in the dark room. The closed window drapes hid any view of the weather outside. Peeking through a slit in the drapes, I noticed that it wasn't raining. It looked liked it could be the beginning of a beautiful day in May. I would soon celebrate my tenth birthday.

While Dad was busy doing other chores, I loaded the wheelbarrow with two empty ten–gallon milk cans, two pails, and two milk stools. Dad opened the heavy wooden gate leading to the pasture, where our small herd of black and white milk cows was peacefully grazing. Dew was heavy on the grass. Birds were chirping and searching for twigs or straws of dead grass to build their nests and raise a family of baby birds. Everywhere was the evidence of new life hurrying to show off the colors, smells, and beauty of an early spring day.

Dad pointed to one of the cows he wanted me to milk. He was never talkative in the morning. I sat down on my milk stool with the bucket firmly lodged between my knees and began milking.

It was then that I first heard the unfamiliar sounds. They were far away, and I couldn't identify them. Rarely was there any traffic this early in the morning. But now I could hear the sound of a truck engine coming down the road from the direction of Surhuis-terveen. I stopped milking and looked toward the road, straining to see.

Suddenly, there it was: not just one truck, but five or six. These

Sietze and his dad miling cows in the pature, 1940.

were not ordinary transport trucks. They were green, canvas–covered vehicles—military vehicles—and they were not paying attention to any speed limits.

I heard a distant explosion, followed by the deep, droning sound of many engines. I knew they must be airplanes, but I couldn't see any. I knew these were not like the regular KLM airplane that used to scare me while flying over our house once a day.

I looked in the direction where Dad was sitting, milking a cow. He looked back at me, but neither of us spoke. We both knew something highly unusual was happening. This peaceful spring morning had taken a scary twist with those eerie sights and sounds.

War

Dad quickly loaded the filled milk cans onto the wheelbarrow, and we headed for the house. The remaining morning chores of feeding the pigs, chickens, and horse were delayed. I followed Dad inside, where he promptly turned on the radio. He stood as if he was glued to the floor while waiting impatiently for the radio tubes to warm up.

Finally we heard the announcer's voice, with its mixture of somber seriousness, excitement, and anxiety. Mom, who was setting the breakfast table, seemed to freeze into still frame as the news came over the airwaves. Hitler's armies and air force, the Luftwaffe, had crossed the borders of neutral Holland. Cities had been bombed. Many innocent people were dead and dying.

There had been talk that sooner or later, Adolph Hitler might decide to turn his armies loose on the Netherlands. But the Netherlands had declared its neutrality, and many Dutch believed Hitler would honor the declaration. That trust was shattered on May 10th, 1940, when the Germans arrived.

All my fears about Adolph Hitler and his deadly airplanes had now become very real. I thought about Mr. Nobach and the praise he had given Hitler while we were talking in the field. Would he still welcome Hitler into the Netherlands now that he had killed our countrymen? The carefree world of a ten–year–old had abruptly been replaced with a world where I would never again feel completely safe.

After breakfast, Dad reached for the Bible, as he did every morning. It was such a regular custom that we kids rarely paid much attention. Usually, the serious expressions on our faces mostly reflected our pretension that we were listening. This morning was different.

Dad read from Psalm 42: "Though an army shall rise up against me, I will fear no evil, for God is with us."

I listened to every word of that reading and every word of the prayer that followed. The dark clouds of war now hung over our country and over my life and the lives of my family. Would I survive? For how long? Would we get bombed? Would my little brother get killed, too? My sisters and parents? I was afraid. All the security and predictability of our daily existence was gone and replaced by an enormous fear of the unknown.

I looked for a place to pray and sat down behind the barn, where no one could see me. Looking up into the sky, which had always been peaceful, I tried to see beyond the danger and hostility created by enemy aircraft. Far above that menace was God. Kneeling, I talked to God, praying for the safety of my family and for an end to the war. But I had a frightening feeling that this day marked the beginning of much worse to come.

As the days passed, Dad and Mom continued listening to the radio for news about the war. We learned that the airplane engines we had heard while out in the pasture were the sounds of the German Luftwaffe attacking Rotterdam in the very early morning hours. The Germans had surprised the Dutch air force by flying over the northern part of Holland, where we lived, to the North Sea, and then turning to approach the coast of Holland from the west instead of the east as expected.

During this initial attack on Dutch airbases, the Germans succeeded in destroying eleven of the twelve Dutch fighter planes that were parked at the Bergen airfield. On the first day, fifteen of the approximately 125 Dutch aircraft were destroyed on the ground.

Before daylight that same day, German parachutists had also landed near Rotterdam and The Hague, capturing important bridges and airfields where reinforcements could be landed from transport planes soon after daylight. Many German nationals and Dutch Nazi sympathizers actively supported the German invaders. French ground forces who came to the aid of the Dutch were forced to retreat only two days later. As the remainder of the Dutch army withdrew, Queen Wilhelmina escaped to London, and her daughter, who would later become Queen Juliana, fled to Ottawa, Canada. She would live there for the remainder of the occupation.

In spite of the terrible strike at the Dutch air force on May 10, over the next five days, Dutch airmen destroyed one third of the entire German air fleet engaged in the air war over Holland—328 of about 1,000 German Luftwaffe airplanes. I learned later that this was an achievement that would never be matched during the entire war. The number of German aircraft shot down and destroyed by the inferior Dutch military aircraft was an indication of the fierce resistance put up by the Dutch air force.

Despite the brave resistance of the Dutch military, it soon became clear that the Germans had infiltrated Dutch intelligence with spies. By the time the war broke out, they already had an exact fix on the actions of the Dutch forces. On the morning Rotterdam was being bombed, the head of the Dutch air force was on his motorcycle heading for his command post after hearing that the Germans had not honored the neutrality of his country. But before he even arrived at his post, he was killed by a sniper. Time and time again, high officials of the Dutch military were picked off by snipers who knew exactly what was going to happen.

Much of the Dutch effort was foiled very early on May 14, 1940. First, the German authorities demanded a cease fire from the Dutch military. When the Dutch did not immediately respond, the Luftwaffe bombed Rotterdam again that evening, leveling the business section of the city and leaving 30,000 civilians dead and many thousands wounded. The attack demonstrated the overwhelming power of the Luftwaffe and led to the capitulation of the Dutch military authorities. General Winkelman officially surrendered late on May 14, and the Germans took over our country.

The end was announced on the radio, along with the many casualties among the Dutch military and its heavy cost to civilians as a result of the indiscriminate bombing by the Luftwaffe. By the end of the five–day war, the official total killed in the military was close to 3,000, with nearly 7,000 wounded and approximately thirty missing in action. The losses for the Germans were almost twice that, serving as a testimony to the fierce resistance of the poorly trained Dutch military forces, who had not been prepared for combat because they had believed Hitler would honor their neutrality. They put up a fierce fight and, given the circumstances, did very well.

Living in the northern province of Holland, we were a long way from the action and the bombing in Rotterdam, South Holland. However, we couldn't help but wonder if and when the conflict would reach our peaceful town. Mom was worried that Dad would be called to active duty at any moment and be forced to fight against the Germans. I was worried, too.

As the German forces settled into Holland, daily life began to change. New rules and regulations were immediately implemented, including the requisitioning of all guns and radios. Over time, rations and curfews further restricted our freedoms.

Even so, the Germans remained rather friendly at first. Hitler hoped that he would be able to win the hearts of the Dutch so he would have no problem with the annexation of the Netherlands to Germany.

He believed in the importance of racial purity and intended to create a completely pure race of white Arians. This group would be known as the *übermenschen*, the superior people, while all others were the *untermenschen*, the inferior people. Hitler regarded the Dutch as pure white Arians and believed they would match the Germans quite well, but he did not count on the fierce sense of independence that the Dutch had and still have. It was clear within a very short period of time that underground resistance was beginning to mount, and with each attempt by the Germans to tighten up on the Dutch, resistance became stronger and stronger.

In accordance with the new regulations, Dad took our practically new, shiny Blaupunkt radio to the courthouse to turn into the German authorities. However, he immediately bought another old radio from a dealer who had never registered it. Although I wasn't supposed to know about it, my parents listened to this secret radio regularly. During the occupation, the two remaining official Dutch channels were completely dominated by German propaganda.

Instead, my parents listened each day to the BBC broadcast from London, which included encouraging messages from Queen Wilhelmina to the Dutch who had the courage to listen secretly. Initially, the queen's escape had been regarded by some as an act of cowardice, but she would have an enormous influence on the Dutch resistance, inspiring her countrymen to resist the Germans in every way possible.

Dad also turned in his sharpshooter pistol, which had been registered when he bought it. But he also bought a clandestine pistol that had never been registered. I knew that these items were secret, things that no one was supposed to know about.

All animals had to be registered, as well. The registration of animals was done by Dutch officials, most of whom were likely sympathizers with the occupation forces. Interaction with these officials stayed on a reasonably friendly level at first. Before the inspector came, I helped Dad hide a little pig in a box–like corner of the pig barn, which also housed the horse. Dad had sworn me to secrecy, because when the inspector came to count all the pigs and other livestock, we didn't want him to discover our secret oinker. They wouldn't be able to requisition for German consumption a pig they didn't know we had.

It was not discovered, and we butchered it once it had grown to a reasonable size. The butcher came one evening and butchered the pig for our family and other family members who didn't live with us. We also used some of the meat to barter for clothing and other food items that were scarce during the rationing. All food items were rationed during this time.

Despite a curfew that was imposed by the Germans, different people began coming and going at our house day and night. Gradually, I realized that my parents were among those involved in the underground resistance movement. I began to wonder how many of our neighbors and townspeople might also be involved. Most remained passive in the hope of staying out of trouble and not exposing themselves to any more danger than what was already ever–present during wartime.

Many others were forced to go underground to escape the authorities after committing some infraction against German rule. They would assume different names and identities and find places to hide during the day, going outside only under the cover of night. Only later did I learn that some of the people visiting us at odd hours were seeking asylum. Often, my mother or father would take them to an interim safe house where someone would be willing and able to accommodate them.

The Way It Was

I remember one young man in his early twenties named Geert Meyer, who lived in our town. He showed up at our house dressed like a lady, with a lot of makeup and a wig. Wearing this disguise, he traveled around on his ladies' bicycle during the day, hoping to avoid being picked up by the Germans. He was a little too brazen, I think, and it wasn't too much of a surprise when he was subsequently picked up and arrested. He was taken to a concentration camp in Germany and never returned. His mother was surely devastated over the loss of her only son for all of the remaining days of her life.

Despite my curiosity about all the activity, I kept my secret knowledge to myself and never asked questions. I had never before had to worry about keeping secrets. But now I worried about the likely consequences if the Germans were ever to find out about our secret guests or our illegal gun, radio, and pig. I had heard about a kid's father who had been killed by the Germans when he was caught listening to a Dutch language broadcast from the BBC on a radio he was supposed to have turned in to the German authorities.

Would they catch us, too? I could not possibly know the answer to that question. All I knew was that I would be the best secret–keeper any ten–year–old boy could possibly be.

A few weeks later, I went to visit Grandpa and Grandma Hoekstra for the first time since the Germans had arrived. I called them Pake and Beppe because they were my mother's parents. Pedaling my bicycle along the path toward Kortwoude was more difficult that day because of a stiff breeze, and I was heading straight into it. It was already early summer, but you wouldn't know that judging by the weather.

After turning onto the road leading to their house, I was pushed by a strong crosswind, which gave me some concern. Alongside the road was a deep, wide ditch, almost like a small canal, and I didn't think I would enjoy it much if the wind blew me into the canal. It reminded me of the story my cousin Tollie Hoekstra had told me about Pake.

War

The incident had happened many years earlier. Pake was a small farmer, but he loved doing a little dealing in cattle. This required him to cover long distances on foot, going to various cattle markets. Sometimes he would walk all night to get to the market early in the morning. After much encouragement, he had decided to learn to ride a bicycle. Finally he had mastered the skill of balancing enough to stay right–side up.

Now he was ready to go to market in style for the first time. He was dressed in his traditional black, puffing lustily on his pipe, which was his constant companion. Since he needed both hands to maneuver the bicycle, he had tied his cane to the bracket leading from the seat to the handlebar. As he neared the bend in the road less than a mile from the house, he suddenly saw the canal. He negotiated the bend in the road but must have been transfixed by the awful possibility that he would head straight for the canal if he failed to straighten the handlebar. Sure enough, bicycle and Pake both plunged into the canal.

When Pake surfaced again, he wasn't even spitting and sputtering. His pipe was still firmly clenched between his teeth, and he was sucking on the stem mightily, hoping that a little spark might be revived. But the drenched tobacco wouldn't light, and Pake never touched his bicycle again.

I couldn't help but giggle as I dismounted my bike and knocked on the door of the small house where they lived. They were already in their eighties, and I didn't see them very often. Pake had a scoop of chicken grain in his hand as he opened the door.

"Oh, hello, Sietze. Come in, boy. I was just going to feed my twenty chickens." He turned around and yelled to Beppe, "Sietze is here, and he's going to help me feed the chickens."

The tiny chicken coop was attached to the house, but there was also an outside door. The chickens were all excitedly aflutter, knowing their lunch was about to be served. Hanging from the low ceiling was a big hunting shotgun. I knew Grandpa had been an avid hunter, but I didn't know he stored his gun in the chicken coop.

"Pake, why is your gun hanging from the ceiling?"

"Well, Sietze . . ." He paused a moment and glanced at the gun, which was hanging with the barrel pointing upward. A small rope had been attached to the trigger and then ran through a couple of pulleys to the outside door. "I'll tell you. Two weeks ago, somebody broke into the coop and stole two of my chickens. I think I know who it was, and I think he's going to try to do it again. So I rigged my gun to go off when anybody tries to open the outside door to my chicken coop."

"Will the thief get killed right away, Pake?"

Grandpa laughed. "No, he won't get killed, but he'll wind up with his pants full. And Sietze, you know what?"

"What, Pake?"

"He won't enjoy cleaning his dirty pants as much as he would plucking another one of my chickens."

Grandpa and I were both laughing as we came into the living room. Grandma had already poured me a cup of tea, in which she had dropped a nice chunk of crystallized sugar. It gradually melted and made the tea even sweeter than one of Beppe's cookies. It was a wonderful treat. But today she gave me two cookies, and I smiled approvingly.

"Sietze, you had your tenth birthday not so long ago," she said. "Congratulations."

I had forgotten about my birthday already. That had been on the thirteenth of May. But it was wartime now, and nobody thought about birthdays much. In fact, there had been no celebrations of any kind. It was a time of great uncertainty.

"Did you have a little party with cake, Sietze?"

"No, Beppe. Dad and Mom listened to the radio for news about the war. Different people came and went all day long. Mom was worried that Dad would be called to active duty at any moment and forced to fight against the Germans. I was worried, too."

I took a sip of tea and a little bite of Grandma's delicious cookies. Grandpa and Grandma both sat across the heavy, tablecloth—covered table, looking at me. I could tell they wanted to ask me questions about what may have happened at our place after the end of the five—day war. I think they knew I wanted to enjoy my cookies and finish my tea so I could suck on the remaining part of the hard—crystallized sugar lump.

War

A little while later, riding home on my bicycle after visiting Pake and Beppe, I thought about all the questions Grandma had asked. I had told her about the radio and gun that Dad had taken to the authorities, but I left out the part about the unregistered ones he had bought to replace them. I did tell her about the little pig that I had helped Dad put in a separate little pen. I knew we were part of her family, and during wartime she worried about every member of her family. I hadn't really lied to Grandma, but I hadn't told her the whole truth, either. It wasn't that I didn't trust Grandma. Some things I just knew I needed to keep secret.

As I approached the house, I saw that the baker was there. His bicycle, with a square basket attached to the handlebar, was leaning against the brick wall. The man came regularly, and Mom would buy some bread and often ten raisin buns. They cost a penny a piece in 1940.

He was in the house talking with Mom and Dad about the only topic of conversation: the Germans and the war. Dad could never refrain from disclosing his intense dislike for anything associated with Hitler's National Socialism movement. But the young man peddling bread and buns didn't know that.

As I walked inside, I heard him say airily, "Well, we're living under the Germans now. We might as well get used to it and jump through whatever hoops they tell us to jump through. Ah, it won't be so bad."

Dad stared at him contemptuously. "It sounds like you are about to join the German army."

"No, I hope not. But if that's what they want me to do, the Bible says we have to obey those in authority over us."

Now Dad was really getting into it. After all, he knew the Bible better than most and did not need a gutless, Nazi–sympathizing bakery vendor telling him what the Bible said. His voice immediately rose to a higher pitch and volume level. Geert, Dad's hired man, was cleaning milking equipment in the pump house and could probably hear the whole conversation.

"Listen," Dad said, straightening up his six–foot frame, "our Queen Wilhelmina is in London, crown Princess Juliana is in Ottawa, and our government is intact. That is the God–given authority we are to obey. That's the authority that tells us to resist the German occupation of our neutral, sovereign country in every way we can."

The man didn't respond. Instead, he got up from his chair and headed to the door.

"It sounds like our government shouldn't have high expectations of you or your kind," Dad added.

As he opened the door to the pump house to return to his bicycle, the vendor gave Dad the best response he could think of: "Baron, I would rather be a live German than a dead Dutchman."

Geert quickly nodded his head in vigorous agreement and said, "Me, too."

Dad's focus immediately turned to his hired man. Scornfully, he glared at him and said, "Geert, did you say that you'd rather be a live German than a dead Dutchman?"

In spite of Dad's blue eyes glaring at him angrily, Geert confirmed that this was what he had said. Dad practically exploded.

"You are a miserable, dirty, rotten coward!"

Perhaps it was the presence of the bakery man witnessing the scene that gave the otherwise passive and quiet Geert courage. Or maybe it was Geert's agreeable nature; now that he had agreed to something, he didn't want to backtrack. He advanced a step toward Dad and said, "What did you just call me?"

Dad repeated the insult. Geert was livid now. Quick as a flash, he took off one of his big wooden shoes and advanced toward Dad, who still had his hands in his pocket but may have been fidgeting with his pocketknife.

"You don't dare say that again!" Geert yelled.

"You are a miserable, rotten coward!"

Geert raised his wooden shoe. Suddenly, the bakery man jumped in between the two warriors and prevented the situation from getting out of hand. Geert put his shoe back on and headed across the field to the place where he lived with his parents.

War

The bakery man climbed on his bike and headed down the road toward another potential client. All of us returned to our activities, no doubt pondering the events that had just transpired. I thought that Geert probably was a coward and wondered how he would react if German soldiers were shooting at him.

I didn't know then that someday I would find out.

# BRIGHT LIGHTS, BRIEFLY

Except for the Germans confiscating all radios and handguns, as well as taking inventory of all the livestock on our little farm, life soon returned to a semblance of pre–war normal. Even Abe, the cattle dealer, came occasionally. Mom often invited him into the kitchen for a cup of coffee and a piece of Frisian cake.

Abe, who was normally a jovial man with an easy laugh, was talking to Dad and seemed in serious, deep conversation. When he got up from the kitchen chair to leave, I heard Abe say, "Baron"—he never called Dad by his first name—"I may not be around too much longer."

Dad said with some surprise, "What makes you say that, Abe? You're not that old, and you look healthy. I don't think the Germans want you in their factories at your age. What are you worried about?"

"I hear that Hitler wants to do away with all Jewish people."

Dad looked surprised. "Are you Jewish, Abe?"

Abe turned while seating himself on the bicycle seat and said, "*Ja, Baron, ik ben een Jood* (I am a Jew)."

With that, he waved his hand in farewell and started pedaling along the sand path leading to the main road. Dad looked surprised and sad as he waved goodbye to Abe. He may have sensed even then that he would never see Abe again.

Every month, I was designated to bike over to the county courthouse in the town of Grootegast to pick up certain food–ration coupons. I hated waiting in line for hours but understood that rationing coupons would increasingly become a fact of our lives under German occupation.

Despite the long lines, everyone remained patient and cordial with each other. The people at the courthouse were all in the same boat and disliked the new rules as much as I did. They just wanted to get their ration coupons. Conversation revolved around the fact that everything was rationed now under the Germans. The only way anyone could get anything was with the coupons that were issued, and those were in limited quantity and only for those with families. Even then, there wasn't nearly enough to feed the families well.

There was also an underground market in goods and services. The Folkerts family were good friends of ours and owned a clothing store in Opende. Like other merchants, Mr. Folkerts had been coming to our house for years with two large suitcases full of clothing. He would unstrap the suitcases from his bicycle and carry them into the house. Mom would then clear the table and meticulously examine any garment or cloth that attracted her interest.

After the war started, we bartered for clothing by supplying the Folkerts with some meat from the hidden pig we had butchered on the farm. Because I had to churn milk every now and then to make butter, we would also exchange butter with some people for other things that the family needed.

In general, however, the market was quite tightly controlled by the Germans. We all had to be careful about what was being handed out, since it was all strictly prohibited and top secret. We never talked openly about it.

Even electricity was being rationed. An inspector came by regularly to check the power meter, and if we had exceeded the allotted number of kilowatt–hours of usage, he would shut off the electricity to our place and seal the meter with a little lead seal and a steel wire, which some people managed to foil. The limited electricity created an especially difficult problem when we needed to milk the cows in the barn during the dark winter months.

Somehow, early in life, I had become attracted to the mysteries of electronics, and now that interest was turned toward some of the challenges on the farm.

One evening, what I considered a bright idea struck me as I was riding my bike along the path, which was nicely illuminated by the small electric light mounted to the front of the bicycle. A small dynamo generated the electricity as its drive shaft wheel pressed against the side of the rotating bicycle tire. I figured I could wire a couple of small lightbulbs behind the cow stalls in the barn. However, I knew I wouldn't feel like setting my bike on a stand with the front wheel slightly elevated and then pedaling for a couple of hours. Although it would be one way of getting out of milking, I knew it wasn't a good idea. I would have to come up with a different plan.

What if I modified the front end of a discarded old bicycle? If I could make a big propeller, I could utilize wind power and mount my invention on top of the barn. I decided to talk to the blacksmith in Opende, who shoed horses and repaired bicycles.

Blacksmith Lubbes was a short but powerfully built man. He was always kind, friendly, and helpful. He was intrigued by my idea of an electricity–generating machine built out of old bicycle parts. Blacksmith Lubbes had a huge graveyard of beyond–repair bicycles. However, one problem completely stumped him: how and where I could get a big propeller to make the wheel turn when the wind blew.

After dinner, I explained my frustrations to my parents. They were never too excited about my endless supply of wacky ideas, but this electricity thing had a practical side that may have prevented them from discouraging me.

When I explained that neither Mr. Lubbes nor I could think of any way of acquiring or making a propeller, Dad looked puzzled for a moment. Then he said, "I'm sure a wooden shoemaker could carve a nice propeller for you out of a piece of lumber. One of our neighbors just two places over makes wooden shoes. He's a nice man. His name is Roel Eilander."

Suddenly, Mom broke out in hysterical laughter. Puzzled, we both looked at her.

"What's so funny?" asked Dad.

"Oh," she said, still laughing and wiping her tears with a dish towel, "that reminded me of what Roel's wife Effie told me last Sunday afternoon."

Dad's curiosity was piqued. Mom could tell that Dad wanted to know what Roel's wife had said that was so funny. Now she looked at me, almost embarrassed. I could tell she really didn't want me to hear. I put on my most naïve expression and waited for her to satisfy Dad's curiosity.

"Well," she began, "Effie told me that Roel takes a bath every Saturday evening in his big, deep wooden tub in the pump house. She said, 'You know, my Roel has a big stomach. He hasn't been able to see his toes for at least two years. When he's down in his wooden bathtub, he can't see his toes, either. The last time he took a bath, he yelled for me. I didn't know what his problem was. I don't generally go and admire my Roel when he's taking his bath, but maybe he had a problem. So I ran to the pump house and yelled, "I'm coming, Roel. What's the matter?"

"He said, 'Effie, come here. Watch the water and let me know when you see bubbles rising.'"

Now Mom and Dad were both laughing, and I slipped out of the house before I started laughing, too. I wanted Mom and Dad to think that I hadn't really caught the joke. At the same time, they had given me a good idea. Maybe Roel would make a propeller for me. I simply had to get up the nerve to go and ask him.

It took me a while to work up the courage to ask Roel Eilander if he could carve me a propeller for my power plant project. Finally, after school one Friday afternoon, I visited Mr. Eilander. I was sure I wouldn't catch him sitting in his wooden bathtub. I had carried my half–finished project along to show him why I needed a propeller to make the wheel turn and generate electricity.

Mr. Eilander was a large, hard-working man. Making wooden shoes was just a side business to help him supplement his day-labor job income and feed his family. I showed him my project and explained the purpose of my visit. He became enthusiastic about the prospect of such a contraption actually working.

"Sietze," he said, "that might work if you mount it on the roof so it will automatically swivel with the propeller into the wind."

I told him that I had already cut out a piece of thin plywood resembling the vertical stabilizer on the tail of an airplane.

"Sietze, that will have to be a big propeller. I will have to carve two sections and attach them both with glue and dowel to the center hub. It will take me a few evenings. Why don't you come back next week, after school on Wednesday?"

I was delighted and thanked Mr. Eilander at least three times.

The following week, I headed home with a beautifully carved propeller under my arm, eager to complete my project. We were deep in the fall season, when light was needed.

To make the situation worse, the German authorities required us to cover all windows every evening with black, wood-framed tarpaper panels. The purpose was to make sure that Allied pilots could not get a visual fix on their location by referencing the lights of towns. The rule was strictly enforced; not even the flickering light of a lantern could be seen from the outside. If German patrols saw a glimmer of light within a house or barn, they would fire a bullet though the window.

The covering of the windows was a very important task every day, particularly in the winter, fall, and spring. It was my regular evening task to cover every window with the black tarpaper panels. I didn't cherish the thought of having a German bullet crash through a window, so I carefully ensured that not a sliver of light would be visible from the outside.

Now I needed to be especially careful, since I expected the inside of the cow barn to be brightly illuminated by the three small lightbulbs wired to my bicycle generator, which I had mounted on the roof earlier in the afternoon.

There was a gentle breeze, and the propeller easily weather–vaned into the wind and promptly started rotating the bicycle wheel. Since we didn't need electricity during broad daylight, I attached a long rope to the vertical tail. This rope reached all the way to the ground and allowed me to rotate the device by walking the rope around the house until the propeller was pointed in the direction opposite from where the wind was blowing. That did the trick and prevented the propeller from turning.

The area behind the cows was dimly illuminated by the feeble light of a kerosene lantern. Dad was already hand–milking the first cow.

"Heit, are you ready for bright lights?" I asked.

He glanced at me with a skeptical look. I knew he was curious, but he certainly lacked confidence in my youthful engineering ability.

I went outside and loosened the rope. The unit turned, and the propeller began to spin rapidly. The wind had really picked up. I ran into the barn and flipped the little toggle switch I had installed in one of the two wires. Immediately the bulbs illuminated. Even the eight cows looked around with surprise. Dad's eyes lit up, a smile crossed his face, and he nodded approvingly.

That night, I dreamed of devices that could be created to sabotage some of the German installations that were appearing everywhere. In my dreams, I created elaborate plots and devices that I would use to sabotage their bunkers and buildings and accomplish much more than merely irritating the German soldiers. They would never suspect a little boy! But I would have to make sure never to brag about my huge successes. I would never be able to tell anyone. That night, I was truly the hero of my own dreams and totally oblivious to the stormy winds howling outside.

It would be morning before I discovered that my marvelous electric– power generator plant had completely blown off the roof.

The next day, with pencil in hand, I sat at my desk in the classroom of my small school. I stared out the window, where the leaves and branches of the large oak tree were moving vigorously. The strong wind, which had blown my ingenious power plant off the roof during the night, was still howling. How could I have attached my invention to the roof more securely and avoided the overnight catastrophe?

I wasn't paying much attention to the teacher. I wasn't much interested in what she had to say, anyway. It was only when I didn't hear her voice that I noticed the silence. Glancing at her, I saw her glaring directly at me.

"*Achtung!*" she said in a stern voice. That was the German word for "attention."

This teacher was new at our school. She had come from Germany to teach us the German language. We didn't like her. Actually, we didn't like anything about the German invaders. Our class was determined not to make this young German teacher feel very comfortable. We pretended to be completely incapable of understanding and pronouncing simple German words. She was quite patient, however, so some of us decided to demonstrate our hostilities in less subtle ways.

After school, she would walk about a quarter mile to her apartment. I conspired with some school buddies to surprise her with a little serenade as she walked to her apartment. We collected pockets full of small gravel stones and hid in the ditch along the road. Patiently we waited until she had completed her after–school work and headed home. Peering through the jungle–like bushes, I could see the door of the school.

"She's coming," I whispered to my buddies. "Shhh. Be real quiet, but get your ammunition ready. I'll let you know when to fire."

We each reached into our pockets and retrieved a handful of gravel. She took short but rapid steps, totally oblivious to the spying eyes of three naughty schoolboys. Now she was directly opposite our hiding place in the ditch. I counted the steps.

"One, two, three, four, NOW!" I whispered hoarsely.

A barrage of gravel stones hailed down on the unsuspecting victim. The ambush hit her with total surprise. She paused and quickly glanced in our direction, without seeing anyone.

As another salvo headed her way, she decided to run as fast as she could. That was a comical sight. She was probably only in her late twenties, but she was short and had the most awful bowlegs I had ever seen. We suppressed our laughter until she was safely out of sight. Not wanting to walk past her apartment, we took a different way home that evening.

It wasn't long after our gravel serenade that the German teacher left our school and returned to Germany.

It was a beautiful early winter morning. The cows were milked, fed, and watered. I had fed the horse, the pigs, and the chickens. Now the family was gathered in the kitchen for breakfast.

I looked out the frosted window. A thin layer of snow covered the roads and fields, the branches, and the few surviving leaves. Smoke from the nearby Boersma home chimney curled straight up, completely undisturbed in the quiet air. It was one of those idyllic winter mornings when the freshly fallen snow glinted in the sun like silver–speckled satin.

Someone was coming down the bicycle path. Straining to look, I recognized Mr. Dalmolen. He was not only the mailman in Opende, he was also the local PTT—Post, Telegraph, Telephone.

Dad went to the door, and Dalmolen handed him a single envelope. There was no postage on it; it was a telegram. I watched curiously as he returned to his chair at the table, opened the envelope, and scanned the brief message. Then, without a word, he placed his elbows on the table and covered his face with his large hands.

None of us spoke. We all knew that whatever the message, it could only be very bad news. After what seemed like a long time, Dad removed one hand from his face and slid the telegram across the table in Mom's direction.

Her hands shook as she unfolded the paper and read the message. With tears in her eyes, she looked at her husband, then to her children. In a choking, nearly inaudible whisper, she said, "Uncle Hans had an accident. He fell off a wagon loaded with bales of straw and landed on his head. He died in the hospital in Groningen." Hans had been only forty–two years old.

We all sat around the table in stunned silence. Dad still held his head in his hands. He had not only lost his only brother, he had lost his best friend. A million memories undoubtedly cascaded through his mind.

There was a story about his brother that Dad had told me many times. He had been seven years old, and his brother nine. He was laughing almost painfully because his older brother had taken him down and delighted in tickling the daylights out of him. It was hard for him to talk. But he felt himself getting stronger every day, and it would only be a matter of time before he would be able to wrestle his older brother down, sit on him, and tickle him.

"Hey, boys, that's enough horsing around," came the stern voice of their father, who had just finished feeding the chickens. "Jeen, you feed the two calves. Hans, you take the bucket and feed the hog," the voice commanded.

The brothers knew very well that such orders were not to be ignored. This was part of their daily chores. If they failed to do it only once, there would be no excuse to shield them from their dad's punishment for being irresponsible. Quickly the boys disengaged and went about their assigned tasks.

My father had also told me about the enormous poverty in their home village and all neighboring villages in 1906, when he and Hans had been seven and nine years old. Farm workers lived in sod shacks consisting of one room that would have to accommodate the parents and children, including cooking, eating, and sleeping. Work was available only during busy farm work seasons.

My father and his brother, however, were scarcely aware of the hunger and desperation of so many families living nearby. They had been born on a small farm, where there was always plenty to eat. Unlike so many others, they didn't have to steal just to stay alive.

I learned later of an upset between the brothers that had occurred during the worldwide depression of the early 1930's. At the time, "survival of the fittest" wasn't easy, even if you had a small business or operated a small farm. Bankruptcy always lurked right around the corner.

It had begun looming closer for my father because his brother Hans had chosen not to buy dairy feed from him any longer. A larger competitor from Grootegast had offered to sell Uncle Hans hundred–pound sacks of feed for a nickel cheaper than Heit could sell it for. Hans lived on a good–sized farm in Lutjegast and was an important customer for my father. Besides, they had always remained close friends, enjoying each other's company whenever an opportunity presented itself.

My dad had sat down behind his small desk to write an angry letter to his brother Hans. Didn't Hans know how hard it was for my father to make a living for his family? Sure, Hans had a family too, but he had a much larger farming operation. He had married much younger, and his children were older.

Hans, I'm very disappointed in you, my father had written. *Don't you know that the Bible teaches that our first responsibility is to our family members? Now your dairy feed business goes to someone who is not even a member of the Gereformeerde church. You should be ashamed of yourself.*

"This is the kind of message Hans needs to hear," he had said somewhat smugly before mailing the letter.

It was several days later when he received a scathing response from Hans. Didn't Jeen realize that the responsibility to provide for the family weighed equally heavy on Hans? Didn't he realize that times were hard and poverty was all around, and how hard it was for Hans, with a wife and three children, plus another baby on the way, to make ends meet? How could Jeen possibly think only of his own interests and be blind to his brother's struggles to make ends meet? How selfish could he be?

My father sat in his chair for a long time, reading and re–reading the letter from his brother. For several more minutes, he stared into space. Abruptly he stood, took his coat off the rack, jumped on his bicycle, and headed for Lutjegast. He was going to face his brother eyeball to eyeball.

Nearly three hours later, he returned to Opende, humming a familiar psalm while the words undoubtedly floated through his head:

Bright Lights, Briefly

How good and pleasant is the sight
When brothers make it their delight
To dwell in sweet accord.

All was well between the brothers again, and they remained best of friends until death parted them. They had since seen each other often, gladly making the hour–long journey on bicycle.

Soon after receiving the telegram, we went to visit Hans's family. They had some children who were about my age and lived on a large farm.

After they lost their father, my dad became a sort of overseer and care-taker of the family. When Dad went down there, I would often go along and look at those kids with a great deal of sadness. Their deep sorrow over the loss of their father was reflected in their faces and in every activity on the farm. I hoped I would not have to mourn my own father's passing for a very long time.

 **DANGEROUS SECRETS**

On my way home from school one day, I saw Mr. Nobach coming on his bike. He frequently rode his bicycle the two miles from his home to his field, usually carrying a pitchfork or tool for whatever work he needed to do on his field. I had seen him working his land next to our house occasionally, but I hadn't talked to him since we had watched that airplane leaving four white vapor trails high in the sky. That had been right before Hitler's German forces had attacked and invaded Holland.

I was just going to give him a slight wave of my hand in greeting and was surprised when he jumped off his bike and said cheerily, "Hello, Sietze. How are you doing?"

I didn't really feel like talking to him, so I muttered a shy, "Okay."

"Well, Sietze," he said, "Hitler is our Führer now and soon will conquer all of Europe, including England."

I didn't respond. I just looked at him and nodded feebly.

"Sietze, I know you've been playing war games in the dark with some of your school buddies."

I tried very hard not to let the surprise show on my face. How could he have known about our secret war games?

"Oh, Mr. Nobach, we're really just playing hide–and–seek. It's fun, especially when it's almost dark. Some kids get scared when we quietly sneak up on their hiding places."

"But Sietze, you use make–believe guns, don't you?"

How did he know that? "Oh, they're just little pieces of pipe attached to a little block of wood. We blow little wads of wet paper out the end of the tube."

"That's quite ingenious, Sietze. You know, in about a year or two, you will be old enough to join the Hitler youth program. It's part–time while you go to school. You get a uniform and learn all kinds of exciting things. Then, in another year or so, you could get into the German army or Luft-waffe with an advanced rank."

My head was spinning. The only thing I was interested in preparing myself for was the Dutch underground resistance movement. I certainly wasn't going to tell Mr. Nobach about that.

Putting on an artificial expression of interest and excitement, I said, "That sure sounds a lot more exciting than playing our little hide–and–seek war games."

Mr. Nobach got back on his bicycle and said as he departed, "You're a bright boy, Sietze."

I continued on my way home, pondering endlessly how Mr. Nobach could have found out about our war games. Was there a traitor among my buddies? Still deep in thought, I arrived home. I decided not to tell my parents about my encounter with Mr. Nobach.

I recognized the bicycle parked against the brick wall of our house as that of my first–grade school teacher, Miss Schipper. As I came into the living room, Dad and Mom were in serious conversation with Miss Schipper. When Dad asked me to go outside and pull some weeds in the garden, I knew that something serious was afoot. I was long out of first grade and had always liked my teacher, so the private meeting couldn't be about me. Maybe it had something to do with the Germans or the underground. Maybe my curiosity would never be satisfied.

That all changed the following day.

Sitting at my classroom desk, I found my thoughts wandering constantly. I wasn't paying much attention to the teacher. Fortunately, Mr. Gorter was a kind and patient man. Otherwise, he would have given up trying to teach me math fundamentals weeks earlier. In the past, I had occasionally had a fleeting thought that I might be the brightest kid in the class. But when I realized that the other kids had no problems understanding what the teacher was explaining, the notion of being the brightest left me for good.

I gazed out the large classroom windows that looked onto the line of oak trees alongside the school building. My mind kept returning to the events of the previous day. It wasn't so much the unfulfilled curiosity about the serious conversation Miss Schipper had been having with my parents, or Mr. Nobach knowing all about our little war games. I may have been able to chase those thoughts away and concentrate on the math lesson. But recurring thoughts of the frightening events that had happened in the middle of the night overpowered my feeble efforts to concentrate on math.

I had awoken to the sounds of someone outside in the dark, knocking on the windows. This had never happened before. Were they German soldiers, coming to take my dad away? My brother and I were sleeping in the alcove bed built into the wall of the bedroom where our parents slept. When they went to bed, they always closed the doors to our bed. Now, fully awake with my heart pounding, I opened the door just a little.

There it was again, much louder now. Someone was knocking on our windows. I heard my dad jump out of bed, excitedly calling, "*Aaf, aaf.*" Mom also jumped out of bed, and I could hear them struggling to get into their clothes in the dark bedroom. All the while, the knocking continued on different windows.

I woke my younger brother. "Listen, Henk. Someone is outside, knocking on our windows."

He sat up and listened sleepily. Sure enough, there it was again, even louder now. Someone was hammering on our windows. Henk grabbed my arm. He was suddenly wide awake and shaking with fear.

"I—I'm scared," he said quietly.

I was scared, too, but I needed to act brave. I didn't want Henk to panic and start crying or screaming.

"Do you think they're German soldiers coming to take Dad away, Sietze?"

It was my own worst fear, but I couldn't let on. "No, Henk. I think if they were German soldiers, they would have knocked the window out with their rifles and jumped into the house." That made sense, and we both started breathing easier.

We heard a key turn the front door lock, and for the next hour we strained to listen to hushed conversation. We could hear Mom and Dad talking, as well as one other male voice I could not identify. Clearly, our parents had let someone in who seemed to be visiting in the middle of the night. Eventually, Henk and I drifted off to sleep again.

When we awoke the following morning, I said, "Henk, don't say anything about what we heard last night. We'll pretend we didn't notice anything."

Mom had prepared our breakfast plate, and everything seemed normal. We didn't appear to have company. Dad was still milking the cows, and Mom went quietly about her work.

"Sietze!"

It was the voice of Mr. Gorter, bringing me back from my anxious thoughts.

"Sietze, you've been daydreaming all through class. I want you to stay after school so I can check to see if you've heard me explain anything about angles and square roots."

I hadn't heard anything about square roots. Of all the roots I knew, none of them were square.

"O—Okay, Mr. Gorter," I stammered, knowing full well that this entire class period had escaped my attention. Now, after school, my stupidity would be exposed. At least the other kids would have left the room by then.

There was one complication. Mom had told me that I should stop at barber Kuperus' shop after school to get my haircut. We didn't need appointments with barber Kuperus, but I didn't want to get home too late because of staying after school and getting my hair cut on the same day.

Dangerous Secrets

After school, Mr. Gorter spent at least half an hour with me. By the time I arrived at the barbershop, there was only one customer ahead of me. He was already in the chair getting his hair cut.

What stopped me was the unusual sight of a German soldier with a big rifle sitting directly behind the man in the barber chair. The soldier was leaning forward, his right hand resting on his rifle, which had been placed on the floor with the gun barrel pointing straight up. He eyed me briefly and then continued his conversation with the man in the barber chair.

Quietly I sat down, listening curiously to the conversation. The German soldier was doing his best to talk in the Dutch language. When he addressed the man in the chair as Herr Nobach, I immediately knew who the man was. He was a brother of Mr. Folkert Nobach, who had talked to me just the day before.

I had heard many stories about the man but had never seen Piet Nobach, who was now getting a haircut. Piet was taller than his brother, with pale blue eyes that were slightly bug–eyed. His cheeks sagged, and his hair was thinning. I didn't like the expression on his face.

The Germans had given Piet Nobach a powerful position in our part of the province of Groningen. He was much feared by the population and had turned in many citizens to the German authorities when he learned that they were not fully complying with all the new German demands.

Barber Kuperus would probably have preferred to cut off Piet Nobach's head rather than his hair, but he didn't show it. He responded to Piet in a kind manner, as if Piet was simply one of his customers, despite the German soldier sitting right next to him.

This was a definite sign of changes in our little town: Piet Nobach getting a haircut with a fully armed German soldier as his personal bodyguard.

I came home much later than expected that day, and Mom was waiting for me.

"Sietze, I want to talk to you for a minute," she said.

Mom waiting for me to come home from school was unusual, and it took me by surprise. Geert, Dad's hired man, was busy loading up the wheelbarrow in preparation for heading out into the field to milk the cows. Mom took me over to where Dad was busy getting the feeding buckets ready for the calves and pigs.

"Sietze, we want to talk to you alone," she said, meeting my curious gaze with her clear blue eyes.

I knew I had not committed any punishable domestic crime. I could also see that the expression on my parents' faces did not reflect anger so much as fear and anxiety.

"Sietze," Mom continued, "you noticed yesterday that Miss Schipper came to our house. You noticed that she was serious and wanted to talk to us without the children present. Did you find that unusual?"

"Yes, Mem. I was going to ask you, but I haven't had the chance yet."

Dad had turned from his activities, and the three of us sat down on overturned calf–feeding buckets. I didn't know where my brother Henk or sisters Betty and Greta were. Clearly Mom and Dad wanted to talk to me alone.

"Sietze, we're going to tell you very important secrets, and you have to promise us that you will never tell anyone. You think you are strong enough to keep secrets?"

I saw the serious expressions on the faces of my father and mother, and I knew this was not a lighthearted matter. This would have something to do with the war.

I nodded my head vigorously, and Mom continued.

"Miss Schipper has one brother. He was a police officer in Heerenveen. He was also not only active in the underground resistance movement, he was the leader. The Germans trusted him because he was a good police officer.

"One dark night, he and a small group of men were in a field where a British aircraft parachuted a shipment of weapons for the Dutch resistance movement. He was caught by the Germans and barely managed to escape before they could execute him."

Wide–eyed, I sat unmoving as my mother told me about the heroic actions of Miss Schipper's brother. "Did they catch him again?" I asked.

"No, but they are looking for him, and if they find him, they'll kill him. That is why Miss Schipper was here." Mom paused and looked at Dad, who seemed deep in thought as he sat on the overturned bucket. "Sietze, Miss Schipper asked if we could hide her brother on our little farm. She was desperately worried about the life of her only brother. Dad and I both know how dangerous it is hiding someone wanted by the Germans, but the Bible doesn't say that we are to love and help our fellow human beings only when it is not dangerous. That's why Dad and I decided to help save the life of William Schipper."

My mouth fell open. A policeman was coming here? The Germans were looking for him? They would kill him if they found him? This was scary . . . but also exciting.

"When is he coming, Mem?"

"He came in the middle of the night—last night." That answered all of my questions about the events of the previous night. "Now, Sietze, if Folkert Nobach or any other German sympathizer finds out that we're hiding someone from the Germans, they will turn us in, and the Germans might kill all of us. They do that when they find out that a family is hiding someone they want. They often kill the whole family, even parents and babies."

I could feel the hair rise on the back of my neck. A tingle went down my spine as I contemplated that awful possibility.

"Folkert Nobach knows all about the little war games us kids have been playing," I blurted out before thinking. It was the awareness of the consequences of Mr. Nobach finding out about Miss Schipper's brother, combined with a host of other fears, that made me add, "And today I saw Piet Nobach, too."

Dad suddenly stood up. I could tell he was worried.

"Sietze, Piet Nobach is a very dangerous man," he said. "Both his sons are with the German SS troops. And you can't trust his brother Folkert, either. Folkert owns that piece of land." He pointed to a rectangular piece of pastureland located between our house and the house where our uncle and aunt and Boersma cousins lived. "Folkert is often looking in our direction to see if he can spot something unusual. We depend on you never to say a word about this to anybody. We have already talked to Betty. Greta is too young, and we thought that you could best explain to your younger brother why we suddenly have company. His underground name is Wim Visser."

Mom added, "Be sure to impress upon Henk that we will all be killed if he should ever tell anyone."

"What if somebody sees him with us?" I asked.

"No one will see him," Mom replied, "because during daylight hours he will always stay inside. We have fixed up a special hiding place. If the Germans come looking for him, he might still escape. In about three weeks, it will become more complicated, because then his wife and daughter will come join him."

After the little family meeting, Dad joined Geert in the field, milking the cows. I went looking for my brother. I had a lot of frightening things to tell him, except that they were now very real. I felt important, like I was already a member of the Dutch underground resistance forces.

Suppertime was only one hour away. I knew that Mr. Visser would be with our family at the table. I would have to prepare my little brother.

Henk stayed with me after we talked, quietly helping with the pre–supper chores. He was no doubt trying to absorb the scary details I had just revealed to him about our new guest. When I said that the Germans wanted Mr. Visser dead or alive, Henk had looked at me with wide eyes reflecting raw fear. I warned him, as Mom instructed, that if anyone knew that Mr. Visser was hiding at our place, he and I, Mom and Dad, and our two sisters would probably be killed by the Germans. I knew Henk would never say a word about our "guest" to anyone. The possibility that our whole family might be killed was too terrifying to contemplate. If the Germans ever found out about our underground Mr. Visser, it wouldn't be because we had talked.

We took our places around the table. The only unusual thing was that Mom had pulled closed the curtains that covered the outside windows. That way, no one from the outside would be able to look in.

Then our bedroom door gently opened, and a tall, strongly built man entered the kitchen. He smiled and shook hands with Betty, Henk, myself, and little Greta, introducing himself as Wim Visser. He didn't look at all like his sister. He had a pleasant look on his face. His eyes were keen and soft blue, but they were also penetrating, as would befit a police officer who could stare a hole right through any suspect.

After supper, we played dominoes while sitting around the table. When darkness arrived, Mr. Visser went outside and smoked his pipe as he walked around the yard. I wondered if he still had his police uniform and his gun. If he did, it was well hidden, because there were few nooks and crannies in our place that I didn't know about. I knew where Dad's pistol was hidden, as well as our secret clandestine radio, although I kept that knowledge from my parents. I had seen Mother crawl underneath the floor of a cupboard bed to secretly listen to the radio. Wim Visser also became a regular listener.

At certain times of the day, the BBC, broadcasting from London, would transmit coded messages for the Dutch underground. Mother may have been familiar with these codes, and she may have passed along that information, because she would often go away on her bicycle. I was sure that whatever she was doing, it had something to do with her involvement in the resistance movement. Only later in life did I realize that she was indeed a frequent courier, disseminating information secretly to other known members of the resistance movement in our area of the Netherlands.

She also distributed clandestine papers, which were secretly delivered to our house for Mom to deliver to various other contacts in the vicinity. About twice a week, we would get a package filled with copies of the small–format underground newspaper called *Orange*—a reference to the Dutch royalty, the House of Orange. I didn't know where the newspaper was printed, but I knew it was distributed only by secret couriers to people who were highly trustworthy or affiliated with the underground. My mother, and occasionally my father, would take a bike ride in the evening to deliver the newspapers to specific people in town. To whom and how many, I had no idea.

The Way It Was

Unlike my parents, most citizens of our country did not have the courage to become active in the resistance movement and hide people like Mr. Schipper, who was wanted dead or alive by the Germans. Although it was frightening, I admired my parents for risking their lives for what they believed. I was determined to be just like them and join the resistance as soon as I turned eighteen.

In the meantime, I knew that these were all dangerous activities, making it important that our daily lives appear outwardly normal, with nothing out of the ordinary.

CONFRONTATION AND RETALIATION

Even during the war, people needed some comic relief to break up the tension now and then. Young boys like myself and my friends created our own. It helped us to think about something other than rations, secrets, and tarpaper–covered windows for just a little while.

School picture. Sietze right with brother Henry and sister Bette left.

The day after Wim Visser arrived, Mr. Gorter once again wanted to spend a few extra minutes with me after school to help me understand the fundamentals of mathematics. He was surprised when I understood the subject matter very quickly, once I concentrated and listened to his explanations. In kind words, he told me that I was really just wasting his time.

"Sietze," he said, "now I know that if you only concentrated and paid attention in class, you would not have a problem with your assignments. It's only because you're daydreaming when you should be listening that you make me have to spend extra time with you and get home late to my family." He looked me sternly in the eyes. "I'm not going to do it anymore.

The Way It Was

If I see you daydreaming in class and not completing your assignments, I'm going to give you failing grades, and you can just sit here in this classroom right by your desk for a whole extra year! If you make me waste another hour of my time, you are going to be wasting a whole year by taking this grade over again. Do you understand?"

I stammered humbly, "Y–yes, s–sir," and left to go home, determined not to get failing grades in class. It would be humiliating to fail and spend another year in the same class with kids that were a whole year younger. Besides, I knew that if I paid attention to the teacher only half the time, I'd have no trouble getting passing grades.

Just as I reached the main street, known as the Groninger Straatweg, I saw an old fellow coming from the direction of Kornhorn on his bicycle, weaving from one side of the street to the other. I recognized him immediately; it was Bouke Peuter. He was always unsteady on his bicycle, always drunk, and always chewing a wad of tobacco. It was comical to watch old Bouke Peuter. He needed the entire width of the paved road just to ride his bicycle. If he heard a motor vehicle approach, he would dismount his bike and lean against a tree until the hazard had passed. He must have hated trucks and cars, even though they were rare in Opende at that time.

Sure enough, along came a German military vehicle. A short distance away, I noticed a couple of my school pals still lingering on their way home. I yelled at them and motioned for them to come to where I was. They came running. It would be much more fun to watch the antics of Bouke Peuter with some fellow mischievous school buddies. Meanwhile, Bouke was trying to get on his bike again. He couldn't have any idea what was in store for him.

My friends Eise and Tiete joined me, and we doubled over with laughter as we watched drunken old Bouke Peuter's futile attempts to get back on his bicycle. The alcohol circulating in his brain and bloodstream no doubt interfered seriously with his sense of balance.

Then he saw us laughing at him. I had heard our hired man, Geert, curse mightily when a recalcitrant heifer kicked him in a very sensitive area, but that was mild compared to the string of profanity old Bouke now unleashed. Chewing his tobacco, he apparently decided that he would just push the bike a short distance to the Wijma Café.

He veered to his left, teetered for a moment, then leaned on the bike momentarily to steady himself before parking it against the brick wall of the tavern. From a short distance away, we watched him intently. He looked around and took a few steps to test his vertical stability. Seemingly satisfied, he spit his wad of tobacco in his hand and carefully placed it on his bicycle seat. After figuring out that the front door to the tavern swung inward rather than outward, he disappeared inside.

A naughty idea immediately jumped into my head. Clearly, old Bouke intended to reuse his chewing tobacco after finishing another gin or two. Tiete and Eise hadn't seen Bouke preserving his tobacco plug for later use. I quickly explained to them that his wad of used chewing tobacco rested on his bicycle seat.

"Eise," I said, looking at my friend, "why don't you find something that looks somewhat like chewing tobacco?"

Eise and Tiete laughed, and Eise said, "You mean, like something that has gone through a horse once?"

It was very easy to find some recycled oats along the Groninger Straatweg in the early 1940's, and it wasn't long before Eise and Tiete had a reasonable facsimile of a wad of chewing tobacco. Tiete added a little moisture. Soon, both Eise and Tiete had dirty, smelly hands. The imitation tobacco looked truly authentic, even to eyes unaffected by alcohol.

I quickly sneaked over, flicked the real wad off the bicycle seat, and replaced it with the nearly identical–looking wad of oats that had gone through a horse. All we needed to do now was stand at a safe distance and watch the drama unfold. Eise was giggling constantly in anticipation of a surprised Bouke Peuter. Tiete stayed in the back of our little group. He had always been shy, quiet, and nervous.

Finally the tavern door opened. I stretched out my arms horizontally, pushing both Eise and Tiete back half a meter to increase the safety distance slightly.

Bouke stopped momentarily on the landing just outside the door to look in both directions along the street. There was no traffic, just three boys a short distance away. He nearly fell as he stumbled down the three steps leading to street level. Approaching his bicycle, he swiveled his head in our direction, quickly scooped up the wad, and put it in his mouth.

As he started to chew, everything seemed to move into slow motion. Staring straight ahead, he lifted his head slightly and stopped chewing. Then he started again, followed almost immediately by a glance in the direction of the three boys who were watching him in anticipation only ten meters away.

He let out an unearthly bellow and started spitting mightily in every direction, yelling repeatedly, "Damn bastards!"

We were practically doubled over in laughter. Bouke wiped his mouth with his elbow sleeves, raised his fists, took a knife out of his pocket, and started coming in our direction.

"Come here, you miserable skinny devils! I'm going to cut your throats."

We were still laughing, but we did back up a few feet. Old Bouke Peuter's threat didn't really scare us, because we knew we'd be able to outrun him easily. The drunken man wheeled his bicycle in our direction, still swearing and spitting. I think he knew we'd be able to outrun him, but if he got on his bike, he just might be able to catch one of us.

Eise was looking around for an escape route as Bouke attempted to swing his right leg over the bicycle seat. Looking scared, Eise said, "Here comes Big Berga."

Berga was the police officer in Opende, a giant of a man, taller, bigger, and stronger than any other grown–up I knew. He was feared by all the naughty, trouble–making boys in town, as well as the misbehaving adults. He looked at the three of us as he dismounted his large bicycle. We were not known as frequent offenders and always tried to look completely innocent. That

Police officer Berga.

was probably why his tone of voice was not combative when he said, "What's going on, boys?"

At that moment there was a crashing sound, and our attention, including Officer Berga's, was focused on a spitting, kicking, and cursing Bouke Peuter sprawled across his bicycle in the middle of the road. Berga immediately turned his attention to the drunken man and helped him get back on his feet as we watched.

"What's the problem, Peuter?" asked Berga. "Did you have one too many again?"

"No, no, no, no, Berga. Those damned, rotten, skinny devils over there"—he pointed in our direction—"they stole my plug of tobacco and gave me a wad of *hynste stront* (horse shit)."

Big Berga laughed with incredulity and said, "Peuter, how could that possibly be? You're just stone drunk."

We started on our way home, laughing all the way.

I had the greatest distance to go and soon found myself alone. It was already early evening. A wispy veil of clouds floated in from the direction of the North Sea, gently enfolding Opende in preparation for another approaching night.

Or were those clouds a harbinger of new wartime dangers ahead?

After I had covered all of our windows with tarpapered frames, I went into the house, where Mom was busy preparing the evening meal. Something was obviously bothering her. She seemed agitated, with a worried expression on her face.

"Is something wrong, Mem?" I asked.

She plunked herself onto a chair and released a deep sigh. "*Ja*, Sietze. You know Dad is an elder in the church. Today, when he was with one of his dairy feed clients, he ran into Piet Nobach. You know Nobach is also a member of our church. He doesn't really come anymore since the war started and he became a traitor. The elders have talked about excommunicating him from the church. But they feared reprisals, and no decision was made other than that he would not be allowed to participate in the Sacrament of Holy Communion. The elders all hoped that he wouldn't show up. Well, today he told Dad that he wanted to partake of communion next Sunday."

"Did Dad tell him that he wouldn't be allowed to?" I asked.

"Yes, and you know, Dad is always straightforward and told him that he was a traitor to his own country and his own people. He accused Piet of turning in fellow Christians if he knew that they were trying to save the life of a fellow human being, even when he knew full well that those people would be killed by the Germans. Nobach roared, 'So, Baron, are you saying that I am a murderer?'"

"Did Dad tell him that he was like a murderer?" I asked.

Mom looked at the window, which was shielded by the dark panel I had just installed. Her hand was shaking, and her voice trembled with fear as she responded, "Sietze, Piet Nobach had a pistol. He pulled the pistol from its holster and fingered the trigger when he said that."

Now I, too, started trembling with fear at the thought of that terrifying scene in the yard of Mr. Pieten's small farm.

"What happened?" I asked, anxiously looking at my mother.

She paused and took a deep, ragged breath. I could just imagine that fearful situation replaying in her mind. "Fortunately, Dad didn't say anything. He turned his bicycle around while Nobach kept yelling at him, and Dad half expected that Nobach would shoot him in the back of the head. Instead, Nobach yelled, 'I am going to get even with you, Baron, you just wait.'"

Mom sighed deeply. Now I understood why she was dreadfully worried. We were especially vulnerable because we were hiding Mr. Schipper. I was scared, too. Nobach could have killed my dad. But he hadn't . . . yet.

Mom raised her head again and looked at me. "Sietze, there won't be school tomorrow."

My mouth fell open. Ordinarily, that would have been music to my ears. Skipping school for a whole day would be a treat. But from the look on Mom's face, I knew the situation was far from ordinary.

Confrontation and Retaliation

"The Dutch government in exile has ordered the Dutch resistance movement to declare a nationwide strike. Farmers won't ship their milk. Factories will close. Only German sympathizers will go to work and open their stores or other places of business. Of course, we don't know how the Germans are going to react. They could come up with some very harsh measures to quell the strike."

That night, I listened to the ceaseless, deep rumbling of a thousand engines as formation after formation of heavy Allied bombers headed toward Germany. But it wasn't just the frightening sounds overhead that kept me awake; it was also the unpredictability, the great uncertainty about our very lives. Finally, while praying to the Almighty who knows all our tomorrows, I drifted off to sleep.

After milking our cows the following morning, Dad placed the milk cans by the road where they could be picked up—but the milk hauler did not come. Many farmers simply poured the milk down the gutter. There was no traffic on the road. Here and there, neighbors gathered along the street to talk. Mom had listened to the BBC broadcast from London and knew that the Dutch strike had seriously compromised German authority.

It was early afternoon when a German military truck, with machine guns mounted on the roof of the cab, roared through Opende. A small group of people had gathered near the street, mostly neighbors, including parents, grandparents, and children. There was a flash of machine gun fire, a hail of bullets. Death. We suffered a brutal terrorist reprisal for the nationwide expression of resistance by the Dutch. My fears and apprehensions about the war coming to our town had been transformed into stark reality.

Freerk Wijma was a friend of my parents who had a family and a good–sized farm. Like many others, he had poured his milk down the gutter that morning. In the evening, Wijma and his young son were busy hand–milking their cows when a German soldier walked into their barn without warning. Noticing streaks of milk mixed with the contents of the gutter, he pulled his pistol from its holster and shot Mr. Wijma in the head. The son looked on in horror as his dying father collapsed to the cement floor of the barn.

The swift response to the nationwide strike left Opende in a state of shock. We now knew how cruelly and decisively the German authorities would respond to resistance. Experiences elsewhere in the country were undoubtedly very similar.

Yet the Dutch were not easily subdued or intimidated. The strike continued. Schools were closed. Streets were strangely deserted. People would sneak through the fields and sand paths to visit friends, neighbors, or relatives. Homes provided some measure of shelter and safety, although there were no guarantees.

With no classes to attend, I discovered that sitting in the house all day was boring for an active thirteen–year–old. All schools were closed, and no one dared to go out on the street.

I was looking forward to that evening when Betty, Henk, and I would visit the Folkerts family. Mr. Folkerts, who owned the clothing shop in Opende, no longer came to our house with his two large suitcases full of clothing. After the war started, even clothing had become scarce. But Mr. Folkerts still came to our house quite often to visit with Mom and Dad. The three of them always fell silent when I entered the room, and I would get the message and quietly exit again. I suspected that the Folkerts were active in the Dutch resistance movement as well.

This evening, we were going to their house to play games and have fun with the Folkerts kids. There would even be a girl about my age, so I was excited. We had to wait until it was dark because the Germans were known to enforce a strict curfew. No one was to be outside after daylight hours.

After the last of the daylight had faded from the sky, we quietly sneaked along the sandy road known as Topweer. It was very dark. There were trees and a ditch on each side of the narrow sand path. We passed the sandy lane leading to the house where Lewis Smits and his family lived.

Confrontation and Retaliation

Lewis helped on our farm during the rye harvest season. He would swing his sharp scythe all day long, chopping the long rye stocks and tying them in bundles.

My sister Betty was nervous. Maybe she had heard some noises coming from the Smits home. The dark silhouette of the house was barely visible; no light from within the house could be seen. Betty made us stop every few steps to listen to a sound she had imagined or look for something she thought she had seen. I refused to use the little flashlight I had in my hand because it was too dangerous. We could be spotted. Actually, it wasn't a flashlight; it was a tiny generator that fit into the palm of my hand. With my thumb I could push a small plunger which engaged a flywheel inside the unit. As long as I kept pushing the spring–loaded plunger, the unit's light bulb would provide some feeble illumination.

Suddenly Betty pulled my coat. "Somebody's coming," she whispered.

We stood stock–still. Our senses were on full alert.

"I don't see anything," I whispered.

Henk said very quietly, "I don't hear anything."

"Listen . . . I hear steps, and they're coming our way," Betty whispered with alarm. "Let's hide in the ditch."

Then we all heard low voices and the vague outline of two people coming down the path in our direction. Fear gripped us; this was serious. We froze, not even daring to whisper. My heart pounded in my chest. I was sure Henk could hear the pounding from where he was standing beside me.

After another minute, we could easily make out the dark silhouettes of two people still moving in our direction.

"Okay, in the ditch," I whispered.

Quietly we slid down the embankment, landing among the tall weeds that filled the ditch at this time of the year. I lifted my head and cautiously peered between the weeds. Betty pulled the collar of my jacket, trying to get me to put my head down.

"Shh," I said. "A man and a woman are coming. They're talking very softly."

I strained to listen. *Oh good, they're not Germans,* I thought, recognizing fluent Dutch. Almost immediately, I recognized their voices.

Spontaneously, probably out of relief, I closed my thumb on the plunger of the little light generator I had been holding in my hand. The brief flicker of light emanating from the tiny bulb caused instant panic. The two people walking along in the dark both jumped, and the lady let out a muffled yell. Betty grabbed both Henk and me while shaking with fear.

"Sietze, is that you?"

The brief ray of light had revealed my face, and the male walker recognized me.

The man's voice was familiar to me. "Yes, Mr. Folkerts, it's me. We were so scared when we noticed someone coming. We're on our way to your house."

We all breathed a giant sigh of relief, and Mr. Folkerts said, "Yes, my wife and I are on our way to visit with your parents."

We had a fun time at the Folkerts' home that evening. We stayed until Mr. and Mrs. Folkerts came back from their visit with our parents. Now we were sure that we wouldn't be meeting any other night travelers on our way home along the dark path.

All the way home from the Folkerts' house, we whispered about the fun time we'd had playing games with the Folkerts kids. There were no scary events during our return, and it was nearly midnight when we arrived home.

As we approached the front door, we heard loud footsteps behind the barn. My blood seemed to freeze in my veins, and my heart skipped a beat. The three of us were taken completely by surprise, for we thought we were safely home. Now, in the blackness of the night, the sound of heavy wooden shoes approached. Suddenly, the dark silhouette of a man appeared around the corner, from between the hog shed and the house. We all stood frozen in place. The man stopped, too, undoubtedly startled by the silhouettes of three young people. Then he seemed to relax.

"Is that you, kids?"

We let out a sigh of relief when we heard Dad's familiar voice. "Oh, Heit, you almost scared us to death," I said.

Dad explained that the hog was delivering baby pigs. Six had already been born, and he was sure more were on the way. Someone needed to watch, because the mother hog would get up after each new delivery, then turn over and lie on her other side. This was very hazardous for the baby pigs already busy searching for their mama's "buttons," from whence they could suck some nourishment. As the mama pig turned, she could easily and unwittingly land on top of one or more of her young offspring, crushing them to death.

"Sietze, it's after midnight," Dad said. "I need to go to bed, but I think two or three more little pigs are coming. Can you watch and make sure the hog doesn't roll over on top of the little ones? You can sleep in tomorrow. Geert and I will take care of the milking, and there won't be school tomorrow, either."

Just as I entered the pigpen, the mama hog was giving birth to number seven. Sure enough, she stood up, sniffed around as if wanting to welcome the new arrival, and then prepared to lie down again. Frantically I shoved the baby pigs out of harm's way as big mama plopped down on her left side. Soon the piglets were all jostling for a "button" again. Now there were seven little pigs and only six buttons on the left side. Then number eight slid onto the straw, and mama rose on all fours again, nuzzled her offspring for a few minutes, and settled down again. I got all the little ones safely out of the way as she lay on her right side. Now there were eight tiny pig snouts jostling for six buttons.

I had asked Dad the year before why a mother hog didn't just have all her buttons in one row. He said that if the hog had all her buttons in one row, the hog would be way too long. I remember laughing at the mental image of a very long hog with all twelve buttons in a row.

As I watched another baby pig coming into the world, I suddenly got a giant ache on the left side of my abdomen. I really hoped that this would be the last one, but the pain increased dramatically.

Forty–five minutes later, while moaning with pain, I was sure that the last little pig had arrived. The mother hog seemed comfortably asleep, with all her young ones nuzzled against her stomach. I virtually crawled to the house in pain and climbed into bed.

It was almost noon when I awoke, and the pain was gone. While eating dinner—it was the custom in the Netherlands to eat the hot meal of the day at noon – I learned that no more little pigs had been born, and all had survived. I never did learn what caused the pain, but it made the delivery of those piglets an unforgettable experience.

 **THE FORBIDDEN PATH**

After dinner, I wandered outside. The quiet beauty of the early afternoon was marked by eerie silence. No one was working in the fields. No sawing or hammering sounds came from Steffen Dijkstra's woodworking shop a short distance away. No traffic of any kind was on the paved road running in front of Uncle Lykel Boersma's place, not even bicycles or pedestrians. Everyone feared German retaliation for the solidarity of the striking Dutch. I thought about the Wijma kids who had lost their father, and the many other mourning families who were experiencing deep sorrow.

I found my mother in what we called the pump house, cleaning the dinner pots and pans. She was bent over a large pan, scrubbing vigorously.

"Mem, can I go for a bike ride?" I asked.

She stood up and looked at me. I'm sure she saw the melancholic look on my face. "Sietze, it's too dangerous to be seen by the Germans anywhere unless you're working," she said.

"Oh, Mem, if I just bike along the sand path all the way to where Uncle Hendrik lives, nothing will happen to me. It's only for walking, biking, and horse–drawn wagons."

She paused. "Okay, but Sietze, promise me that you won't go on the pavement."

"Okay, Mem."

It wasn't easy riding the bicycle along the path. Bicycle tires were not available during the war years. The strip of hard rubber fastened around the rim of the wheel made riding the bike on a sand path a real chore.

I quickly passed the neighbors' houses, including Old Eare and Jeltje van der Tuin, then Roel Eilander's home and wooden shoe workshop. I rode by a small, forested area known as the Komieze Bos. On the other side of the dirt road from Komieze Bos lived tall Johannes. It was his job to collect the toilet barrels from all the town's inhabitants. Each week he would collect the full barrels and exchange them with empty ones. Even from a considerable distance away, I could smell that tall Johannes had a fresh load of barrels in his yard. The stench was enough to make a spraying skunk look cross–eyed.

At that spot, to make matters worse, the compacted, nearly hard surface of the path turned into soft sand. I didn't have enough pedal–pushing power and had to walk my bike all the way to the farmhouse where Uncle Hendrik lived. As I got close to the paved road, I thought about how easy it would be to ride my bike on the pavement rather than the sand path. A small voice inside reminded me not to even think about it. I decided I would just take a look.

As I pushed my bike, I noticed a dark blue and white magpie bird gathering twigs and heading for one of the large oak trees that lined both sides of the main street between Surhuisterveen and Opende. Magpies, or *eksters*, as we called them, favored the tall oak trees for building their large nests. Unlike other birds, magpies built completely enclosed, predator–proof nest structures. Only a round opening on the side of the nest provided entrance and exit for the parents and their growing offspring. The sounds of the noisy birds seemed magnified in the utterly quiet and peaceful surroundings.

Arriving at the main street, I stayed close to the side of the road. Despite the peace and quiet, I knew that it could be very dangerous being on the road, so I stayed on the grass alongside the road and close to the ditch.

The Forbidden Path

Inching forward, I looked in both directions. The street was completely deserted, with no vehicles, wagons, bicycles, or pedestrians anywhere. On my right was the large Van der Werf nursery. No one was hoeing the weeds, pruning the trees, or tending the acres of plants and decorative trees. On my left was the Avek factory. Dozens of people worked at Avek, but today there was no one in sight. There were no lights visible through the windows and no sounds from the usual noisy machinery. In protest against the German oppressors, the country was on strike. It was eerie.

I felt a heavy sense of foreboding as I stood there and pondered. I looked down the deserted, hard–surfaced street toward Opende. I would certainly be able to go faster here than on the loose sand path. In the distance, I could almost see the house where Dad's sister, Aunt Fintje, lived with her family. Only two small fields of pastureland separated the Boersma house from ours. I could be there in less than five minutes.

Now I looked once more in both directions along the street. Nothing was moving, no danger in sight.

My decision was made. Impulsively, I jumped on my bicycle and started pedaling furiously. Pretending to be racing an imaginary competitor, I made quick progress, biking right in the middle of the brick–paved street. Now the front of the Boersma home was clearly visible. It had been used as a tavern but had closed when the war started. Most of my Boersma cousins lived in the home with my uncle and aunt. When I got there, I would just swing my bike into their yard and push it along the path of the pastureland about two hundred yards to my house.

I was halfway there when I heard something in the distance behind me. My heart skipped a beat as I turned my head to look. A petrifying fear gripped me when I saw what was coming. A large German military vehicle with soldiers manning a machine gun was coming up behind me at high speed. Increasing my pedaling speed, I swerved to the side of the street and looked again.

Instantly, I knew I was going to die. Could I run my bike into the ditch and try to hide? I took one more quick look and saw one of the soldiers swiveling the large, mounted machine gun and aiming it in my direction. Now I knew that they had already seen me. Hiding in the ditch was no longer an option. I had only seconds to live. Maybe I wouldn't even hear the machine gun. The bullets would kill me before the sounds reached my ears.

I had read somewhere that when sudden death seems imminent, a thousand thoughts can flash through one's mind in seconds. I had promised Mom that I wouldn't go on the street. I had been disobedient. Was God going to punish me now? Would Jesus forgive me, or would I go to hell? I didn't want to die. Ever since the war had started, I had hoped to live to be at least eighteen years old. I expected to die fighting the Germans in the Dutch resistance. Now I would just die a disobedient young boy.

I thought about Mom and Dad. Would Mom be mad because I had disobeyed her? No, she would be very sad. I would never see my brother Henk again. I knew he would feed my rabbits for me. He would have to sleep alone. I wouldn't be there to encourage him during the night when scary war sounds kept us awake. I would never see my sisters Betty and Greta again. Would they miss me? Would there be a funeral for me? Would they put my bullet–riddled body in a wooden casket just like Jantina? Would all my uncles, aunts, and cousins come to the funeral? Everybody would know that I wouldn't have died if I had only obeyed my mother.

The roaring military truck was close now. The terror that had gripped me moments before dissipated, replaced by a sense of serene acceptance of the inevitable. I slowed my frantic pedaling to a more leisurely pace. The roar of the truck was loud and very close now. I held my breath.

Then, in a flash, the truck passed me. One of the two German soldiers turned his head to look at me. The distance between me and the fast–moving vehicle quickly increased, and I could breathe again. As I released the pent–up fears and emotions from moments before, tears began streaming down my face. Sobbing uncontrollably, I thanked God for sparing my life.

I reached the gate separating our yard from the fields and parked my bike against it. As I was climbing the gate, Mom came running out of the house, her arms spread wide. Still sobbing, I literally jumped into her arms.

"Oh Sietze, I'm so glad you're alive," she said.

The Forbidden Path

Between sobs, I stammered, "I'm sorry. I'm so sorry."

Mom told me that she had been worrying desperately for fifteen minutes, thinking I should have returned home already. Had something happened? She was standing by the window looking for me when the German truck with the machine gun barreled down the street. She assured herself that I would not have gone on the street. Then, finally, she had spotted me pushing my bike along the side of the pastureland.

Shortly after the early evening supper, I asked Mom if I could go to bed. She nodded silently, probably surprised. It was unusual for me to want to go to bed early, and I hated it when I was ordered to do so as punishment for some youthful indiscretion, usually without supper. This evening, I had expected the "to bed without supper" punishment. It was the only time I really knew I had deserved it. I had actually looked forward to it.

Our suppertime had been unusually quiet. I suspected that they all knew about the events of the afternoon, but no one mentioned it.

I was still awake when Henk came to bed. Usually we talked before going to sleep. Sometimes I would spin fabulous tales of imagination that were heroic, scary, or hilarious. Whatever the subject, I usually convinced him that the events had really happened. Tonight there was no conversation, and soon his rhythmic breathing told me that he was fast asleep.

Meanwhile, I tossed and turned endlessly. Terrifying scenes of being ripped apart by big machine gun bullets tortured my consciousness.

After hours of restless slumber, I decided to get up. It was about six in the morning, the beginning of what would be a beautiful sunny day. Sparrows were busy building their nests under the roof tiles. I loved watching the busy birds preparing a safe, cozy home for their young.

Jumping across a dry, shallow ditch, I peered down a hollow shaft going deep into a decaying tree trunk. The shaft was too narrow and too deep for birds of prey like magpies and crows to reach the tiny eggs and baby birds. It was early in the morning, and I hoped the pretty little bird with an orange spot on top of her head might be on her nest, adding another egg to the three I had seen the day before.

To my dismay, only a few twigs and some tiny feathers were all that remained of the nest. I looked around for the bereaved birds. Suddenly, I knew who had done this evil deed. The only person I had told about the nest was my friend Eise. We often walked to school together. He must have destroyed the nest and taken the small speckled green eggs to add to his collection.

Angry and disgusted, I decided I would punish Eise for this inexcusable misdeed.

I strode back to the house and entered the kitchen. The door to the living room was halfway open, and I noticed Mom crawling on her stomach through the small opening below an unused alcove bed had built into the wall. It was the secret hiding place for our clandestine radio, where Mom sometimes listened to the BBC *Radio Orange* broadcast in the Dutch language. It didn't seem to bother her that I knew about our secret radio. We had already been entrusted with life–or–death secrets.

"Sietze," she said, "the strike in Holland is over."

I couldn't tell whether she was sad or glad. Mostly sad, I thought, because the strike had not produced results and had cost many lives. I shivered involuntarily as I thought about my close call the day before and the families, even in Opende, who had lost loved ones.

School would start again on Monday, and I was looking forward to it.

Saturday was never my favorite day because of all the yard chores I had to do. Today's schedule was particularly heavy. I had to hoe and pull weeds in the flower garden, pick leaves off the small lawn, rake the sand path around the house, and spread white sand to give the yard that real spic–and–span look. That was probably mostly for the benefit of people who would take their Sunday afternoon stroll past our house. People had been house–bound all week, and now that the strike was over, they would likely come out in droves for a stroll on a beautiful Sunday afternoon.

I worked diligently but often rested to look at the street. It was clear that things were more or less normal again. There was some traffic on the road again: bicycles, a few pedestrians, a horse–drawn wagon, and an occasional motor vehicle.

"Sietze, it's time to peel potatoes," Mom called from the open door to the pump house.

"Oh, Mem, I've been so busy. Can't Henk do it?"

"Henk will help you. The potatoes are right here in the pump house."

Mumbling my displeasure, I headed inside.

Potatoes for our Sunday dinner always had to be peeled on Saturdays. Mom and Dad strictly observed the teachings and customs of the *Gereformeerde* faith. Dad even shaved on Saturday evenings, never on Sundays. Even our playing activities and games were restricted on Sundays.

Henk came through the door into the pump house with his potato–peeling knife in his hand. He looked far more than just grumpy. Even though it didn't occur to me then, it seems that neither of us enjoyed any form of work that required getting our hands dirty. That seems strange, since we were born to parents whose ancestors had nearly all been involved in farming. Was some divine evolution taking place, informing the embryo that the inhabitants of the planet were easing out of the Agricultural Age?

All I knew was that I hated peeling potatoes. One look at Henk's face told me that he enjoyed getting his hands dirty even less than I did. It would be no surprise when he became a college professor many years later.

With both of us sitting on milk stools, each on one side of the large pan of unpeeled potatoes, I found Henk's grumpy facial expression somewhat amusing. While peeling the first potato, I began thinking of something that would add to his irritation and maybe send him "over the edge." What a naughty thought!

Then an idea struck me, and it was hard to stifle a grin. Yes, that would do it. Poor, cranky younger brother was just about to be sent right over the edge.

Henk had finished peeling his second potato when I commented that his peelings were too thick. Mem always wanted us to peel the potatoes as thinly as possible to minimize waste.

Henk clearly didn't appreciate my criticism and growled something like, "Mind your own business."

I dropped another peeled potato into the pan of water and focused on a large, heavy peel. It had come from a potato Henk had just peeled and was nice and thick. I dug the point of my knife into it and, with one quick motion, flung it at my brother's face. It took him completely by surprise, and before he knew what had happened, a fat potato peel was hanging across the bridge of his nose.

I roared with laughter, impressed by the accuracy of my fling and the comical sight of my angry brother.

"You rotten *mispunt*," he blared. That word wasn't even close to meaning "sweetheart."

I laughed harder still.

The laughing turned out to be my downfall. I hadn't noticed Henk quickly spearing a peel on the point of his small, sharp knife in preparation for returning the favor. Suddenly, out of the corner of my eye, I saw Henk's arm move with a flinging motion. I jerked my head to the side to avoid the projectile.

Unfortunately, I jerked my head directly into the path of Henk's sharp knife, with the peel attached to the tip. The sharp blade slid cleanly across my forehead, instantly transforming it into a geyser of red liquid. Through the blood in my eyes, I saw the panic and terror on my brother's face.

"Mem . . . Mem . . . MEM!!" he yelled with such urgency that when Mom reached the pump house moments later, her blood pressure was already off the scale. Instead of fainting at the sight of my bloody face and blood-stained clothes, she became resolute.

She looked at the bleeding gash just above my left eye and yelled, "Henk, get Geert and have him get Dr. Colett from Kornhorn." Dad wasn't home.

I could hear Henk's wooden shoes literally flying out of the pump house along the side of the barn, yelling with that same level of urgency. "Geert . . . Geert . . . . GEERT!!"

"Oh goodness," Mom said, looking at my wound. "I've got to stop the bleeding." With both hands, she pinched the long gash together.

I heard the heavy wooden–shoe steps of Geert approaching. He took one look at my head and only said, "Ooooh."

"Geert, get Dr. Colett. Maybe someone can call him on the telephone at Wijma's Café. That's the closest telephone. Please, Geert, hurry."

With those words from Mom, he hurried away. I heard him mount a bicycle just outside the pump house.

Mom was standing right in front of me, gently pinching and keeping the wound closed. She kicked the vacant milk stools close together and, without disrupting her tender grip, we carefully lowered our posteriors onto the milk stools. The bleeding had stopped. Henk was nowhere in sight.

"How did this happen?" Mom asked.

I explained the events that led to my now having an extra hole in my head.

"It sounds to me like you started it, Sietze."

"Oh yes, Mem, it was really my own fault. Henk didn't intend to hurt me. Where is he?"

"I don't know. He may be suffering more than you are right now."

I could imagine him on his knees somewhere in the barn, praying for me.

More than an hour passed before the pump house door opened and Dr. Colett appeared, satchel in hand. He took a good look while Mom kept pinching and said, "Mmmmm, pretty good cut. Good thing it missed his eye. Bleeding has stopped. You did a great job, Mrs. Baron."

Mom didn't smile. She just nodded her head. Then he opened his satchel and extracted a metal box, which he opened. Inside, twelve large staples lay in a neat row. They seemed even larger than the staples Dad used to fasten the barbed fence wire to wooden posts.

"Okay, Mrs. Baron. It's a fairly long cut, so I will use four or five staples, and the wound will remain closed without you holding it any longer."

The staples fit in a pincher–like clamp tool. I didn't think much of Dr. Colett. He put five staples in my head, each requiring puncturing the skin above and below the wound. Now I had ten more holes in my head, and the pain and bleeding started all over again. In fact, putting those miserable clamps in my head hurt much more than the nice clean cut Henk had made.

After fastening a large bandage across the now closed wound, he said, "Sietze, you'll be good as new, and in about a week I'll come back to remove the staples."

I thought, *Wow, Doc, that'll give me some more pain in the head to look forward to.*

After paying the doctor ten guilders, Mom helped me get up from the milk stool. She held her arm around my shoulder, probably because she half–expected me to faint on account of not having enough blood left in my head. She installed me in a large easy chair in the living room that was used only when important company came. When everyone gathered around the table in the adjoining kitchen for the evening meal, Mom brought me a plate of food.

"Mem, I won't have to go to church tomorrow, will I?"

"No, Sietze, it's better you stay home with all those staples in your head. Your friends will ask you what happened, and poor Henk will feel so ashamed of himself, he won't dare to look at anybody. And it was really your own fault."

"Yes, Mem. I started flinging potato peels. It was my fault."

I hadn't seen Henk yet. I figured he must be sitting at the table eating, but I never heard his voice. We would still have to sleep together like we did every night.

I went to bed right after eating my soup and bread. Half an hour later, I heard Henk come in very quietly. I pretended to be sound asleep. Very carefully, he climbed over the top of me and looked at my wounded head. Convinced I was sound asleep, he carefully crawled under the blanket on his side of the bed. I knew he was facing me and was probably studying my head intently.

Suddenly, another naughty thought popped into my head. I simultaneously opened my eyes wide, flung my arms in every direction, and yelled, "Ouch! I'm dead! I'm dead!" When I saw the terror on his face, I smiled at him and said, "Okay, Henk, now it's your turn again . . . but be careful, will you?"

I had scared my poor little brother half to death. He stammered, "S– Sietze . . . You rotten *mispunt*."

The Forbidden Path

Then we both laughed and soon fell asleep. All was well again between brothers.

My sore head yielded one significant benefit. For three days, I didn't have to help milk cows or feed the pigs and chickens.

Early on Tuesday morning, Mom said, "Sietze, you have to go to school today. Otherwise you'll fall way behind and stay dumb."

I protested, saying that I didn't think I was dumb now.

"Okay, Sietze, but there is room for improvement. Come here—I'll wash your face carefully. Just tell your buddies that you had a little accident. I don't want the kids in Henk's class to tease him about cutting you."

"Okay, Mem. I don't want anybody to tease my brother, either. If they do, I'll hit them on top of their sorry heads with my wooden shoe."

She smiled a little. "Just be careful. Don't make trouble. You could wind up getting a big, fat, swollen goose egg on your head. That, together with your cut, would make you both dumb and ugly."

Naturally, the teacher was curious about the big bandage on my head. "Sietze," he said, "it looks like you've been in a war. What happened?"

"It was an accident, teacher."

"How did you have an accident?"

"With a knife, peeling potatoes."

The teacher started laughing a little. "Did you try to peel the skin off your head?"

The whole class giggled, and I gladly joined them. Fortunately, that was the end of my interrogation, and I successfully avoided telling the whole story.

Only during the coldest winter days would the kids take a lunch bag from home and eat at school during the lunch hour. Otherwise, we walked home for our main meal of the day.

On the way home that day, I caught up with Eise. He was really my friend, but I had a bone to pick with him.

"Eise, you destroyed that little bird nest in the stump along the Scheiding."

"I wanted the eggs for my collection."

"You didn't have to pull the nest apart, you stinker."

With that, I gave him a good shove, with the intention of making him fall topsy–turvy in the grass alongside the road. Instead, he went topsy–turvy head first into a deep, dry ditch along the road. It was a bad fall. Grimacing with pain and rubbing his neck, he crawled out of the ditch. I had not intended to make him suffer that much, although he had certainly made those nice little birds suffer.

After eating dinner, I hurried back to school again. Henk and I were walking together but were soon joined by other buddies. I told them how I felt a little bad about having pushed Eise in the ditch. They agreed that he did deserve some punishment for destroying the home of a beautiful little songbird family.

My friend Tiete had a habit of looking in different directions. Suddenly, he yelled, "Sietze, here comes Auke van der Hoek on his bike!"

I looked quickly and felt my heart in my throat. Sure enough, there was Eise's dad, leaning over the handlebars to reduce wind resistance and pedaling as fast as he could. He looked enraged and ready to avenge his son's painful descent into the ditch.

Oh man, oh man, I thought, *he'll probably break every bone in my body. Or he might rip the bandages off my head and jerk the staples out with the bandage.* There couldn't be much blood left in my head, but the bleeding and pain would start all over again. Dr. Colett would have to come back with his box of staples. Maybe my head would run out of blood entirely, and I would be dead.

In a desperate panic, I looked for an escape route.

We were almost near the Folkerts' clothing store, but it was still too far. Van der Hoek was almost ready to tumble off his bike and grab me. Scared as a deer when it sees a hunter training a rifle on him, I headed for a barbed wire fence more than four feet high. I would normally never have been able to scale that fence. But with the fear of death in me, I sailed cleanly over the top and raced across the pastureland. I hid in the tall grass until I was certain I wasn't being hunted any longer.

On my way home after school, I walked with Eise, and soon we were friends again.

We were almost at Van Kammen's building business when we saw them coming: two fat German soldiers on bicycles, with rifles slung across their shoulders. They both came to a standstill when they reached us. They didn't get off their bicycles, but rather steadied themselves by touching the toes of their boots on the road.

"*Ich will Wurst kauffen, verstehen Sie?*" said the one.

The other, with his fat rear on the saddle and his feet on the ground, had one of his fingers up his nose. When he extracted it, he examined the retrieved substance on the tip of his finger before flicking it in the direction of the other soldier, who didn't notice.

I felt like saying, "*Schweinhund*," but instead I nodded my head. They wanted to buy sausages and were looking for a butcher shop. My older cousin, Sietze van Dellen, owned a butcher shop in Opende. It was not far away, and there was another butcher shop even closer. I decided to be very helpful and pointed to the main road about a hundred yards ahead. I motioned for them to go straight across that main road until they came to a bridge. The butcher shop would be right there.

"*Danke schön*," they said, then wheeled their bikes around and headed across the main road.

Eise watched the two fat–assed Germans and began laughing.

"Shhh, Eise, shut up," I urged. But as soon as they were out of sight, we both roared. We knew that by the time they reached the bridge, they would be more than a mile away and would realize that there wasn't a butcher shop or any other shop in sight. They'd be way out in the country looking for *Wurst*, while we were safely home.

The Way It Was

Even Mom and Henk had a good laugh when I told them the story. Mom said, "You took a little part in the resistance movement, Sietze. You know, as long as the Germans are our enemies, they have no right to the truth."

I think she wanted to make sure that I understood that lying, in general, was a sin and not acceptable.

 **DEADLY DAYS**

My head healed. Only a scar remained to keep the flying–potato–peel event vivid in memory for the rest of our lives.

Now it was two weeks later, a beautiful Sunday morning. After break-fast, our refugee from a German firing squad, Mr. Visser, excused himself while the rest of the family dressed for church. Sunday was dress–up day. Mom would wear her Sunday best, while Dad put on a suit and white shirt with a stiffly ironed collar and a tie. Mom took a great deal of pride in her family of four children. She made sure they were all neatly dressed before leaving for the fifteen–minute walk to church.

Using the bicycle on Sundays was frowned upon. It was deemed to be more God–glorifying if the twice–Sunday pilgrimage to church was made on foot. Since there was rarely any traffic, we could walk in the middle of the road, often joining other families also on their way to church.

First there was the Van der Veen family, Wiggele and Hinke with their children and the children's grandfather, who lived with the family. One of their kids was about Betty's age, and another girl was about Henk's age. Their grandpa was the merchant known as Little Peter, who supported himself by selling petroleum fuel and prunes from his bicycle.

Hielko Lettinga was also on his way to church. I figured his one leg was a little shorter than the other, because one wooden shoe was built up by several centimeters. Still, he limped a little. He and Eabe De Haan were walking together and talking.

"Eabe, you are a young man," Hielko was saying. "Aren't you afraid the Germans are going to pick you up one of these days and put you to work in one of their factories in Germany?"

"No," responded Eabe. "I'd pretend I couldn't understand a word, and I know with my harelip they wouldn't understand me."

The Westra family was just coming out of their small grocery store–home combination. I left Henk walking with Tryn van der Veen while I joined my friend Jan Westra.

As we walked past the Folkerts' clothing store, the family was just coming out of the house section of the store, and we were quickly joined by our friend Andy Folkerts. As we got closer to the church, the crowd of parishioners increased. Another friend, Hendrik, appeared as the Age Kuperus family joined the throng of churchgoers.

Inside, we all dispersed and sat with our own families while waiting for the service to begin. I indulged in my life–long habit of people watching. There was Mr. and Mrs. Lubbes, the Roel de Vries family, the Van Kammens, the Graansmas, the Leistras, and many more. There was nothing unusual or worth studying about those familiar faces. I knew them and regarded them all as important people.

It was a warm Sunday. Rays of bright sunshine illuminated the members of the congregation and projected grotesquely distorted profiles of some familiar faces onto the off–white painted stucco wall of the church. I made a game of matching a projected profile with the rightful owner of the image. I studied them until Dominee van Dijk came out of the council chambers and mounted the stair that led up to his elevated pulpit.

Following the Dominee were the elders, who seated themselves in a special bench to the right of the pulpit. The deacons followed and sat to the left of the pulpit. The preacher would then announce the singing of a hymn.

Being an elder, Dad sat in front of the congregation with the others. When there was a delay before the music started after the announcement of the hymn, I often noticed him glancing sideways up to the balcony. That was where most of the members of the band Crescendo gathered every Sunday to provide the musical accompaniment to the hymn singing.

The band began playing, and everyone in church stood up to sing the first psalm.

That was when it happened.

Eabe sat one row ahead of us, and I watched him closely as he opened his psalm book. I knew that he looked funny talking with his harelip, and I was eager to watch him sing. When the congregation started singing, he was still turning pages. He must have forgotten which psalm had been announced and tried to look over the shoulder of the lady standing one row in front of him. He craned his neck slightly but couldn't quite look over her broad shoulders.

She was equally broad in the rear, and as he lowered his eyes to return to paging through his book, he noticed something very peculiar. It was warm in the church, and the center of the lady's dress had cozily gone into hiding between her sizable buns. Eabe was a very good–natured man, and it must have been with the best of intentions that he concluded that the lady was unaware of the embarrassing sight of her dress stuck in her rear.

I'm convinced it was his helpful nature that caused him to lean forward slightly and, in one quick motion, pull the lady's dress out of its confinement.

Eabe was totally unprepared for the lady's swift and painful reaction. She would not suffer such indignities kindly. Turning slightly, she forcefully swung the heavy psalter in the direction of the person behind her. The blow caught Eabe squarely in his left eye. I could tell by the grimace on his face that it was a painful blow. He held his hand over the injured eye and dropped the psalter on the bench.

He was still kindhearted Eabe, and he must have thought that the lady was angry because she liked to keep her dress exactly where it was. Had he known that, he would have never pulled it out.

Now the best he could do was to remedy his earlier mistake. He bent forward and began to carefully tuck the dress in between the lady's buns again.

POW!

The psalter hit him squarely in the right eye. I heard him utter a subdued "Ouch!" Now covering both eyes, he sagged down in his seat. Eabe needed to find a balm in Gilead.

Sitting in the pew after the singing, while the preacher was reading from the Bible, I continued looking at Eabe. I was sure he had meant well. It was funny watching Eabe trying to tuck the lady's dress back where it had been stuck, and I snickered a little.

Now poor Eabe was really suffering. The skin around his eyes was deep red, turning almost blue, and he continued to dab at them with his handkerchief.

Just before the start of the three–point sermon, it was time for a long prayer. Since it often lasted up to fifteen minutes, there was a tendency for some church members to fall asleep, especially men who performed heavy labor many hours a day, six days a week.

Of course, it was not appropriate to fall asleep during a church service. Many men would rise and stand during the "long prayer."

I knew I was supposed to keep my eyes closed while the preacher was praying, but I didn't always do it. My chances of getting caught with my eyes open during prayer were slim, because Mom also had to keep her eyes closed. I would always glance first to see if Mom had her eyes closed when I opened mine.

I looked at the man who was sitting in the same bench where we were sitting. Now, during the prayer, he was standing up. His eyes were closed, hands folded across his stomach, droplets of perspiration glistening on his forehead. I watched as his head began to sag lower and lower. Suddenly it would jerk up again, and his eyes would open. This was repeated several times. As his head sagged progressively lower, the man began to sway. Each swing of this tall human pendulum increased, until I was sure he would fall across the lap of Miss Schipper, the first–grade school teacher. Fortunately, the "amen" came before the fall.

During these quiet moments in the church building, I could sometimes hear airplane engines overhead and was intrigued, despite the danger they represented. With a great deal of curiosity, I found my mind wandering as I thought about how the pilots could talk to people, whether their commanders or their control towers from the air, or from aircraft to aircraft. That fascinated me and probably instilled a desire in me that later led me into electronics and amateur radio.

Once the prayer came to an end, Dominee van Dijk began his sermon for the day, preaching about God punishing people for their sins. At one point, he said God had caused everybody in the world to drown, except one family and one of each species of animals. He never explained how and with what Noah fed the tigers, lions, buffalo, and birds. Surely he wouldn't feed one of the sheep to the lions? Did he have enough hay for the cow and the bull, or enough eucalyptus leaves for the Koala bear? Questions like that always came to my mind.

Whenever I asked Dad, he would simply say, "Sietze, if the Bible doesn't explain, we don't need to know."

While listening to the pastor and thinking about Noah and all those animals in the ark, I noticed something very unusual. The janitor was walking rapidly up the aisle on the left side of the church. This wouldn't have been surprising on a cold winter Sunday, when he would have had to replenish the coal–burning stove that heated the church in wintertime. But now he was practically running. With an alarmed look on his face, he quickly walked up the stairs to the chancel where Pastor Van Dijk was preaching. He whispered in his ear, and the pastor's face immediately took on an expression of fear.

Closing his sermon book, the pastor looked out over the attentive congregation and said, "We have just been informed that the Germans are conducting a roundup at churches in the neighboring town. All able–bodied men between sixteen and forty are being rounded up for labor in German factories. Please leave as quickly as possible, not through the front door, but through the council chambers and the rear door. Walk through the fields and stay away from the road. All women, children, and those that are not in danger should leave calmly through the main church doors. The Lord bless you and keep you, the Lord make His face to shine upon you and grant you His peace. Amen."

There was an immediate commotion as men rushed toward the exit doors in the back of the church. Watching my father leave with the other men after a hasty good–bye, I trembled with fear. German soldiers could storm in at any moment and start shooting at the escaping men.

As we waited for our own turn to leave, I thought about my older cousin Reinder Prins, who had been picked up by the Germans and put to work in a German airplane factory. I learned later that he attempted to escape, but the Germans caught him and made sure he would never make another escape attempt. He was ordered to dig a deep hole, in which he could stand up straight with only the top of his head above ground level. The soldiers then proceeded to fill the hole until the dirt reached his mouth and nose, at which point they made him promise that he would never do such a thing again. They extricated him after warning him that if he ever tried to escape again they would fill the rest of the hole completely and bury him alive.

As soon as the men had left the church, all the remaining church members left in the customary way. Mom held Betty and me by the hand. I took Henk's hand, while Greta held on to her older sister Betty. Everyone was quiet and wanting to get home. I thought about all those men walking through the fields and pasturelands, jumping across ditches, heading in various directions to get home safely. Silently I prayed for them.

Hielko, in his uneven wooden shoes, was walking by himself. I had noticed that Eabe, too, had left the church through the back door. Poor Eabe with his sore eyes. I was glad that he had decided, in spite of his eyes and his harelip, that the Germans would still regard him as an able–bodied man.

Dad wasn't there when we arrived home. We knew it would take him longer because he and the others would be forced to keep hiding as they dispersed through the fields and stayed away from the roads. I imagined my father hiding in a ditch and trying to make himself invisible if he saw any German trucks in the distance on his way home.

To everyone's relief, Dad made it home safely. We found out later that all of the men had successfully avoided the Germans. But it was a memorable

Deadly Days

Sunday, reminding us that no place was safe from the occupiers, not even the Lord's house.

Although the trick I had pulled on the German soldiers a few weeks earlier had been amusing, I had since been reminded that lying was a sin. But black–and–white moral principles had become a little fuzzy during this time of war and secrets. Being a part of the underground resistance movement with my parents forced me to face difficult questions, whose answers could determine life or death.

With Mr. Nobach often working his land adjoining our place, there was constant tension at our house.

One day, I had poured three buckets of water into our makeshift boiler. The boiler was a large, round iron tub located behind the pig barn and set on a grill above big chunks of firewood. I had lit the fire and was pushing a wheelbarrow full of potatoes to be cooked in the boiler when I heard, "Sietze!"

Somebody was calling my name, but I didn't recognize the voice. Looking in the direction of the voice, I saw Folkert Nobach casually leaning his arms on the wooden gate that separated our yard from his land.

"Sietze," he called again, motioning for me to come to the gate.

What would Mr. Nobach want from me? I couldn't ignore him. I needed him to keep thinking that I was his friend and a good candidate for joining the Hitler Youth. I put the wheelbarrow down and walked toward him.

He smiled amiably and said, "How are you this beautiful day, Sietze?"

I returned the smile. "I'm fine, Mr. Nobach, just keeping busy with farm work during summer vacation."

"Sietze, boy, I want to ask you something."

I looked at him with an expression that must have said, *Okay, go ahead,* because he continued.

"I saw a lady by your clothesline the other day hanging up baby clothes. It wasn't your mom, and besides, I don't believe you have any babies in the family. I didn't recognize the lady. Do you have company?"

The Way It Was

I tried to keep the smile on my face, but every fiber in my body screamed with fear. He must have seen Mrs. Visser. She and their two–year–old daughter had come several months earlier to live with her husband, who was in hiding at our house. My parents had agreed to help again at the cost of doubling the danger. Mrs. Visser slept in one of the alcove beds at night and ate meals with our family like her husband. But while Mr. Visser was never seen outside in the daylight hours, his wife had not been as mindful of the rule while helping with the chores. Now, here it was—a life or death question.

At that moment, four German fighter planes roared overhead. I stared into the sky, looking at the planes. But most importantly, I needed time to think. Mr. Nobach was also looking at the German fighters. Black swastikas were clearly visible on the sides of the fuselage.

A million conflicting thoughts raced through my head. Should I just tell him the truth? I knew that lying was a violation of God's laws. Besides, Mr. Nobach liked me, and he would surely see to it that my life would be spared. A cold shiver traveled the length of my spine.

The fighter planes were making a giant loop in the sky. No doubt they were searching for easy prey, which usually came in the form of a crippled Allied bomber returning from Germany after being damaged by anti–aircraft fire. Both Mr. Nobach and I watched intently.

If I told him the truth, the Germans would surely kill Mom and Dad, my only brother, and both of my sisters. I would be the only one to survive. Would I want to be alive if all the people I really loved were dead? Would I ever be able to forgive myself, knowing that I had been responsible for my family's death?

Perhaps our whole family could escape. After I told my mother what I had told Mr. Nobach, we could all leave quickly. But where would we go? The Germans would hunt for us and for Mr. Visser. Who would milk the cows and feed the calves, pigs, and chickens? Some of us would likely be captured and executed. Wouldn't God hold me responsible for murder if I told Nobach the truth? Wouldn't murder be worse than lying? Would God consider Nobach entitled to the truth, knowing that he would use it for murderous purposes?

All four airplanes came out of the bottom of the loop in perfect formation and climbed straight up into the sky. They must have spotted a partially crippled bomber trying to make its way back to the base in England across the North Sea.

Mr. Nobach had an awe–stricken smile on his face as he admired the tight formation of the German pilots until they disappeared from sight. I hoped that all the noisy airplane action had caused Mr. Nobach to forget about his question.

"Wow. That's awesome, isn't it, Sietze?"

Putting on my most sincere, agreeable expression, I looked at him and nodded my head vigorously up and down.

"Sietze, those German Luftwaffe pilots are the best trained pilots in the world. Those poor English bastards don't have a chance against the mighty Luftwaffe!" I was still nodding my head in agreement when Nobach suddenly added, "Okay, Sietze, tell me about the lady with the little girl by the clothesline in your yard. Was it one of your aunts?"

With adrenaline racing through my body, I replied, "No, Mr. Nobach, she is not my aunt. She is a lady from Rotterdam. Someone in our church asked my parents if we could put up a lady with her little daughter from Rotterdam. They were starving, and her house was bombed back in 1940. Her husband is working in a German factory. She needed help, and my parents agreed to help her." I looked him squarely in the face, surprised by my newfound boldness.

"That was good of your parents to help the lady. You're a good boy, Sietze. Maybe you'll be a Luftwaffe pilot some day."

I smiled, again nodding my head vigorously. Mr. Nobach returned to his fieldwork while I sauntered shakily back toward the house.

I never did tell my parents about my hazardous encounter with Mr. Nobach. I didn't want to worry them about the possibility that I might say the wrong thing should I be interrogated again.

One day, those planes I had seen in the sky as I talked with Mr. Nobach came even closer to home. Now they would no longer be merely fearful images in the sky, but rather real machines of destruction.

After completing six grades in the Christian school in Opende, I had been deemed a sufficiently promising young student to merit going to high school. Now I had a new routine in the mornings. After helping Dad with milking and other chores and then eating breakfast, I would gather my books and notepads, mount my bicycle, and head for the southern part of Opende. There weren't too many houses in that area of the city. The most heavily populated area was the Juliana neighborhood. That was where Lange Hylke lived with his short wife, Wobbelke, and, of course, the monkey, which helped them provide enough money for Lange Hylke to buy liquor and imbibe. My first–grade girlfriend also lived along the Juliana Lane, but I had lost track of her. She was probably still in grade school.

I dismounted my bike and secured it safely to the stand that had been placed near the small railroad station in South Opende. In the distance I could hear the rumble of the small train, or tram, coming down the tracks, preparing to stop where I was waiting. There were usually very few people who regularly traveled by tram from Opende to the small city of Drachten, where the high school was located. There were only five people in the car when I entered. Most were probably coming from Groningen on their way to Leeuwarden, the capitol city of Friesland.

One man caught the attention of nearly everyone aboard that car. He wore what appeared to be old, badly stained formal wear. A tall stovepipe hat adorned his head. His black, long–tailed coat was a veritable jungle of medals, medallions, and other marks of distinction.

His name was Jan de Roos. He was a street singer known virtually throughout the entire country of Holland, not so much for the power of his vocal cords as for his unusual behavior. It was entertaining to watch Jan de Roos, especially if you dared ask him what a first–place greyhound race medallion had to do with his singing. He would unleash a verbal tirade on any listener who had the "stupid audacity" to toss only a copper penny into Roos's upturned stovepipe hat while he was wiping the perspiration from his brow after another stirring, back–bending performance. He was a colorful character, attracting attention wherever he went.

Today he would be in Drachten, because he exited at the same time I did.

From the railway station, I walked the short distance to the high school, known as the M.U.L.O. It was still a few minutes before the start of the school day, and I noticed a small cluster of boys talking in a corner of the graveled schoolyard. Normally their behavior tended to be somewhat rambunctious.

It was different today. They were talking about one of our classmates named Adrie Klamer. I knew him well; he sat only two desks in front of mine. He was a lively character and the only one in our class who couldn't speak the Frisian language. He lived with his mother in Bergum and arrived each day by a train coming from the other direction.

When his family lived in Rotterdam, a German bomb had killed his father during the first night of the war. Poverty and hunger had driven them to the province of Friesland, where a family helped them with food and shelter.

As I listened, I learned that on his way to school that morning, loaded down with his schoolbooks, Adrie had attempted to jump onto a moving train car. Unable to keep his grasp on the vertical hand rail, he swiveled backward and fell between two cars. He died instantly.

Again, I had to come to grips with mortality and that great finality through the death of a classmate. I struggled with it even as the teacher prayed. He prayed for Adrie's mother, all alone now, her only child taken away. He prayed for Adrie's friends and classmates and for faith in eternal life after death. It was very quiet in class that morning. Students bent over their books, working on the assignment without the usual whispering.

It was early afternoon when our quiet classroom suddenly erupted

Air battles over Drachten

with the piercing sounds of air raid sirens. Everyone bolted upright in their seats. Even as the teacher shouted for us to crawl under our desks for cover, we heard the eerie whistling sound of bombs screaming earthward. All around us was the cacophony of roaring airplane engines, exploding bombs, and the rattle of heavy–caliber machine guns. Through it all came the ear–piercing wail of the sirens.

Although I was terrified, at the same time I was curious to see what was happening. On all fours, I crawled over the hardwood floor through the exit and into the schoolyard.

The sky was filled with aircraft. German fighter planes were attacking hundreds of four–engine bombers on the way to the German heartland. The defense by Allied fighter planes was fast and furious. One moment they were corkscrewing upwards, and another moment they were diving. Sometimes one of the planes would go into a steep dive and then rise straight up, trying to get a tactical advantage on another aircraft. The success of the maneuver depended a great deal on the skill of the fighter pilot.

I lay on my back against the wall of the school building, watching the action with fear and awe. I was fascinated with airplanes and had studied the different types of planes used in the war. Now I saw that a Messerschmitt was desperately trying to outmaneuver a pursuing P–38, with guns spewing hundreds of .50–caliber bullets together with 20 mm. shells from its wing canon. The Messerschmitt was in a near–vertical dive, blazing away with all four machine guns. It looked as if both aircraft might slam into the school in another second or two.

Heavy–caliber machine gun bullets kicked up gravel in the schoolyard not far from me. A huge bomber corkscrewed toward earth in a screaming death dive, crew members tumbling out of the fatally stricken craft. Not all of the parachutes opened. I jumped involuntarily as one uniformed body slammed into pastureland adjoining the school grounds.

The Messerschmitt made one final, desperate effort to climb steeply away from the devastating firepower of the P–38. A moment later, it exploded into a fireball and crashed straight down. I could see the smoke rising from several crash sites.

As quickly as it had started, it was over. Instant death and destruction had loomed so near. Now Drachten returned to life again, and I shakily walked into the classroom as students crawled out from underneath their desks.

After school, I ambled the approximately 1,000 feet to the railroad station and boarded the tram on its way to a stop in Opende. It had barely left the station when it came to an unscheduled stop. I noticed German guards on both sides of the track. No one could exit the train.

Nearly two hours passed before the wreckage of a crashed Messerschmitt was cleared off the tracks and the train once again began moving toward its first regular stop, Opende.

# PREY AND PREDATORS

"Sietze!"

From the tone of Dad's voice, I could tell that whatever he wanted was important. It wasn't his custom to have casual chats with his children. I quickly dropped my garden hoe and walked over to where he was standing.

As I approached, Mom came out of the pump house to join us. *This must really be important*, I thought. Dad seemed worried and uncomfortable. Mom's expression reflected fear.

"Sietze," Dad began, "life is getting very dangerous around here, especially for those known to be involved in the resistance movement. You know we're hiding Mr. Schipper and his family. We know that Folkert Nobach is suspicious."

I nodded my head vigorously, remembering how Mr. Nobach had interrogated me about the lady he had spotted hanging clothes on our clothesline. I had never told my parents about that scary encounter, but I understood the mistrust.

"You know that the high-ranking German accomplice in this region is Folkert's brother, Piet Nobach."

Mom now seemed eager to join the conversation. "Sietze," she said, "do you remember I told you about Piet threatening Dad after Dad had to tell him that the church elders would not allow him to partake of communion?"

I nodded my head, and she continued.

"Piet Nobach has two sons who are both members of the brutal and much feared German SS forces. One of the sons was home on furlough and was hand–milking the cows in the field so his dad could sleep in that morning. Someone from the resistance movement, not knowing that Piet was not milking this morning, snuck up through the pastureland on the unsuspecting cow–milker and shot him in the back of the head, killing him.

"We are expecting terrible retaliation by an enraged father. We have also received a tip that sometime today, the Germans will be conducting a regional manhunt. We hope they will not come to this area, but we cannot be sure. Dad will not be around today. You are too young to be picked up by the Germans, so you will be working today with Kees van Dekken. He is probably still too young to be taken, too, but perhaps borderline."

"What about Mr. Schipper?" I asked.

"He's hiding here," said Mom. "He doesn't have any place else to go. We must pray that danger will not come near."

I worked hard at keeping a calm expression on my face. Inwardly, I was trembling with fear.

"Sietze, we suspect that you know about our secret radio," Dad said, looking at me as if expecting an answer.

Almost imperceptibly, I nodded.

"But we don't think you know about our secret pistol."

Fortunately, he didn't seem to expect an answer. I didn't need to confess that I knew about the pistol or that I knew exactly where its secret hiding place was. I also knew that Mr. Schipper had a pistol, a gun much bigger than the one hidden just below the roof tiles in the straw.

"It's getting much too dangerous to keep those items," Dad continued. "If I were to be captured, the Germans would ask me about such things. If I was to deny it, and the items should subsequently be found, they would not be very easy on me. That's why we want you to take the radio and the gun and bury them somewhere. Make sure it's not an obvious place that could be easily discovered. You must figure out where to hide those items. Mem and I do not want to know where you hid them, and you are absolutely never to breathe a word about their existence."

With that, he reached into his inside coat pocket and handed me the revolver and a small box of bullets. As both my parents turned to go to the house, Mom looked at me and said, "You know where the radio is, don't you, Sietze?"

I nodded, and they left me staring in bewilderment at the sight of a pistol in my hand.

Then it was as if an electric cattle prod jolted me, shocking me out of my state of momentary incomprehension. Quick as a flash, I slid the pistol into my pocket with the bullets, safely keeping my hand on it. Aimlessly I walked into the field, where our cows were peacefully grazing. I looked at them with a twinge of jealousy as one lifted her head and looked at me with those large, trusting eyes, without a trace of anxiety or fear—the very emotions that now threatened to overwhelm me.

I kicked the heavy corner post that supported the wooden gate leading to the field. I needed time to think, time to plan where and how I should hide the secret pistol and radio.

Kees van Dekken was coming across the field, a hay rake slung over his right shoulder. I would be working with Kees today. Even though he was my friend, I couldn't tell him about my secrets.

While ambling back toward the house, an idea struck me. More resolute now, I picked up my pace and entered the house. There was no one around, so I quickly crawled under the alcove bed and retrieved the large wooden radio. Walking through the cow stall area, which was clean now that it was summertime, I grabbed a shovel and slipped into the chicken coop. Much to the consternation of about a hundred chickens, I removed their large, round metal water container and started digging.

Five minutes later, I carefully lowered the radio, which I had placed in a cardboard box, into the hole. After quickly covering the boxed radio with sand, I slid the water container back into place and viewed the result with satisfaction. There was no sign of disturbed sand, and the earth below the water container would never yield its secret.

The pistol in my pocket would be another challenge.

As I was exiting the chicken coop, there was an enormous explosion. Almost simultaneously, a terrific blast of what seemed like compressed, concussive air tore at my clothing. Nearly petrified with fear, I fell to the ground—though I didn't know whether I had been knocked to the ground or allowed myself to fall flat on the grass as a protective reflex. Raising my head slightly, I saw Kees's head carefully rising above the small stacks of hay he had been working on.

"Are you okay, Sietze?" he yelled.

Still shaking, I stood up. "Yes, Kees, I think I'm okay. But what was that?"

He pointed. "Look at all that smoke. It must have been a big bomb."

I noticed the smoke rising high into the air not far away. "Let's go look."

We started walking across the fields in the direction of the column of smoke.

"You know, Kees," I said, "that could hardly have been a bomb. We would have heard at least one airplane. Did you hear an airplane?"

"No. I thought I heard a whooshing sound, and the explosion and monstrous blast almost knocked me down. I thought I was going to die."

We were now only some 1,200 feet from where the smoke was rising.

"I'm still shaking, Kees, but you know what? We didn't hear or see any airplane. It must have been one of those German V1 or V2 rockets."

"Oh, I bet you're right. Maybe it was on its way to London and something went wrong with its steering system."

"I think so. They launch it from a mobile station, you know. That way they can move from place to place and keep the Allies guessing where they are."

"I've seen them go up in the distance many times," replied Kees. "They shoot straight up, leaving a fiery trail. Then, when they're pretty high, they turn in the direction of England, and sometimes you can see a vapor trail for several minutes."

I nodded my head in complete agreement. Then my heart skipped a beat. I had completely forgotten about the revolver in my pocket. Had it fallen out when I hit the ground? If so, it would be lying close to the chicken coop door.

My right hand shot into my pocket, and my heart resumed its normal rhythm when I discovered that the gun was still there. I was tempted to look at it just to make sure it was there, but that fleeting notion was quickly discarded. It was a secret not to be shared with anyone.

Now we were standing at the edge of an enormous crater, wide and deep enough to bury a good–sized house. Remnants of smoking and smoldering V2 missile wreckage were scattered over a wide area. People from every direction were approaching now. Most kept a respectable distance, while others approached very cautiously.

Fortunately, this errant rocket had crashed just along the sand path known as the Scheiding. Other than creating a huge hole and leaving debris on some farmer's land, it had damaged nothing and injured no one. I thought about the poor people in London who were targets of these silent killers every day and night.

Quietly we walked away as more and more people arrived on foot and on bicycles to satisfy their curiosity. Kees looked at his pocket watch. It was close to noon, and since he was near his parents' home, he decided to have lunch before returning to his work.

"Sietze, can you help me put the loose hay into little stacks this afternoon?" he asked. "With all this excitement, I got way behind and won't get it finished before evening. I need to get it done because it's expected to rain tonight."

"Sure, Kees, I'll help you. We'll forget about German rockets and have a good time."

With my hand firmly on the gun in my pocket, I continued on my way home. I was certain that Mom would have the noon meal prepared. But I wasn't thinking about food nearly as much as I was trying to focus on a suitable burial ground for the gun.

My few remaining steps to the house were interrupted by the sound of screaming fighter plane engines. I had neither seen nor heard them approach until they were at rooftop level with machine guns blazing.

Instantly, I dropped face down on the ground, clasping my hands around the back of my head to protect myself. Empty heavy–caliber machine gun shells rained down from the sky all around me and on the ribbed aluminum roof covering the pump house. I had heard hail pelt the aluminum roof and create a lot of noise, but it paled in comparison to the ear–splitting sound of heavy copper machine gun shells.

A blood–curdling scream came from inside the pump house, where my sister Betty had been busy cleaning pots and pans when the barrage hit the roof.

After the threat had passed, I ran to the pump house. At the same time, Mom came running out of the cellar when she heard Betty's screams, thinking her daughter had been hit by gunfire. She and Greta had quickly hidden in the cellar when they heard the attacking aircraft.

Like me, Betty had instinctively fallen flat on her face when she heard the noises. Unfortunately, the surface of the pump house was concrete, and the injury she sustained as a result of dropping face–down had caused her to think that she had been hit. All of us breathed a sigh of relief when we found Betty shaken but in one piece.

Afterward, we learned that two British Spitfire aircraft had spotted a tanker wagon on the street about 900 feet in front of our house. A high–speed dive toward their target brought them right over us, practically at rooftop level, where they commenced firing at their target. The pilots undoubtedly assumed that the tanker was filled with fuel intended for German consumption. It was actually filled with milk headed for the processing plant in Surhuisterveen. Now the milk tank was riddled with machine gun bullet holes, and milk was flowing into the ground between the bricks in the street.

There was no laughter and little conversation as our family sat around the table for lunch, with two empty chairs where Dad and Mr. Schipper usually sat. The fears of the hazards of wartime were all too real and all too close.

———————————

After the noon meal, I quietly walked outside. It was a beautiful summer afternoon. Kees was already raking the hay into neat little rows. Later, he would put his pitchfork into the end of a row and start pushing the hay into a pile. Then, picking a specific point, he would begin pushing hay from the other direction toward the now growing pile of hay. All that remained then would be to neatly round off the tops of the haystacks to allow rain to run off without getting much of the hay wet.

Mentally, I was working hard, too, trying to chase away the gloomy mood that held me in its grip. That was difficult while I was still holding the gun in my pocket with my right hand, knowing that I wouldn't have an opportunity to hide it until evening.

"Hi, Kees," I called out.

He responded and held another rake high in the air, a gentle reminder that I had promised to help him this afternoon.

I took the rake with my left hand and said, "You're doing well. Already eight nicely rounded stacks completed."

"Yes, but there'll be thirty by the time we're finished."

"Did you see those two Spitfires shoot a milk tanker full of holes?" I asked.

"No, when was that?"

"Right at noon. I was just ready to walk into the house when those big fighter planes roared overhead with their machine guns blazing. Empty shells were falling all around me. Man, I thought I was going to die."

"Wow, that's the second time today. We were sitting around the table this morning when I thought I heard some noise. But everybody was talking about the big hole from the German rocket crash, and I didn't go outside.

"Sietze, why don't you keep raking the hay into rows, and I'll stack it into piles. It's supposed to rain tonight, and your dad won't like it if we don't get it done."

"Kees, look up—there's not a cloud in the sky. And besides, Dad isn't home today."

Looking up and visually sweeping the sky from horizon to horizon, he said, "You're right, but that can sometimes change . . . in . . . "

He stopped mid–sentence and stared toward the street where the milk tanker had been strafed. I could see alarm registering on his face. Turning to look, I saw two German covered trucks. One was continuing east toward town, but the other had stopped. German soldiers armed with rifles were jumping out, crossing the ditches, and entering the fields. At this time of summer, many young men were working in the fields. Clearly this was a roundup, a hunt for able–bodied men to take with them and put to work in the war equipment factories in Germany.

"Kees, you've got to hide. They might take you. You're a big, strong guy and look older than sixteen."

German soldiers were fanning out in various directions, and we heard the first rifle fire.

"Okay," Kees said with a trace of fear in his voice. "I'll sit here, and you pitch hay on top of me and make it look just like any other haystack."

I shook my head in disagreement. "Kees, they're close. We don't have enough time. If they suspect that some are hiding in the haystacks, they'll shoot right through the haystacks and could kill you."

Kees was getting nervous and more fearful. Two German soldiers were running through a field with rifles at the ready, disturbing our cows.

"Kees, let's hide our rakes and two pitchforks under the rows of hay. Then you crawl on your stomach under a stack of hay. I'll crawl under another stack, and it won't look like anybody's been working here. If they shoot through the stacks, chances are they won't hit us as long as we're flat on our stomachs."

Kees disappeared under a haystack. I selected a stack a little closer to our house and crawled on my stomach, pushing my way carefully to avoid altering the appearance of the stack of hay.

When I looked toward our house through some loose hay near the edge of my hiding place, my heart pounded. Mr. Schipper, who was hiding from the Germans, stood near the house with his police officer pistol in his hand. He was bending over and glancing in every direction. My brother Henk was not far away, seemingly shaking with fear as he watched Mr. Schipper.

With pounding heart, I started praying. Thoughts tumbled through my head like an avalanche. Would this be the end of our family? Why was our "man in hiding" not hiding now? Perhaps he was sure that they would find him anyway. His wife and little daughter were once again hiding in the cellar with my mom, Betty, and Greta.

Prey and Predators

I reached into my pocket for the gun and took five bullets from the little box. With shaking hands, I loaded the gun. I clicked the safety into the "off" position. German rifle fire was now close by. I moved slightly to look in the direction of the shooting.

Geert, our other hired man, was running across our field at a speed that amazed me. He was zigzagging as he ran, with German soldiers in pursuit. They began firing their rifles and yelling, "Halt, halt!"

Geert kept zigzagging until he tumbled into a ditch. They caught him, slapped handcuffs on him, and headed toward one of their trucks. I wondered if I would see him again. From that moment on, I would always remember Geert as a hero, rather than a coward who would rather be a live German than a dead Dutchman.

Mr. Schipper partially retreated into the corridor of the house. If they found him and he started shooting, they would surely zero in on our house and kill everyone inside. I wasn't going to lie here and watch that happen. I would never be able to live with myself again. If I saw them going into the house, I decided I would sneak up on them and shoot as many as I could.

I clutched the gun tightly. Every muscle in my body was taut with tension as I prepared to burst out from underneath the hay. Instead of peacefully chewing their cud in the adjoining pasture, the cows were all running around nervously. More shots were fired, and more handcuffed men were taken to the waiting covered trucks.

Relief flooded my entire being when I saw the trucks begin moving and driving off. Many minutes later, my breathing returned to normal. Once they were absolutely sure it was safe, the women emerged from the cellar, and Mr. Schipper put away his pistol.

It was dark by the time I finished burying the gun in the field. What a relief it was to finally get the dangerous weapon out of my pocket. I was glad that I had not been forced to use it.

The next day opened with a beautiful sunrise in a clear sky, typical of late summer in Groningen. Nothing in the quietness of that peaceful morning reflected the horrors of war, which were never far away.

I ambled along the sand path, deep in thought and hardly noticing the large marker indicating the border between the provinces of Groningen and Friesland. It was impossible to ride my bicycle, with its solid rubber tire strips, along the sand path. I certainly wasn't going to risk taking my bike along the hard–surfaced road. I remembered all too vividly escaping what I thought would be certain death when German soldiers had trained their machine–gun sights on me. I still trembled at the thought. I was fine without my bike. I wanted time to think, anyway.

"Good morning, Sietze."

The voice startled me. I hadn't seen Mr. Eilander standing by the tall hedge in front of his house. He was standing as still as a sleeping horse and almost blended in with the hedge.

"Good morning, Mr. Eilander," I replied. "How are you? I saw you walking past our house a few days ago when you were drenched from top to toe. What happened?"

Mr. Eilander's eyes grew wide as he told his story. "I was working in the field near my boss when two German Stukas flew overhead, being chased by two American Mustangs. Big machine guns from all four airplanes were blazing. I was watching the scene from near a big oak tree, when hundreds of oak leaves suddenly fluttered down. I realized the bullets were hitting the tree, so I hit the ditch. I didn't think it was deep, and at this time of the year it's usually dry. But it was deep and full of water. I had to walk home and change my clothes."

"You must have dove in head first, Mr. Eilander," I said.

He ignored that. "So, Sietze, the *moffen* didn't get you yesterday, either?" The *moffen* was our name for the German soldiers.

"No. I was hiding with Kees van Dekken. But I don't think they would have taken me anyway, because I'm still too young."

"Oh, you never know, Sietze. From my hiding place, I watched them capture Geert. The Germans are getting pretty desperate. I've seen young boys in German uniforms with large rifles slung over their shoulders, which they seemed barely able to lift."

"You're right, Mr. Eilander. I saw very young German soldiers guarding the train station in Drachten a few days ago."

Mr. Eilander nodded his head in agreement. "Yes, and among the kid soldiers are the gray–haired grandfather soldiers still fighting for Adolph Hitler's crumbling empire."

Two Lancaster fighter–bomber planes roared overhead. Our heads swiveled as we followed the rapidly disappearing aircraft.

"The Allies pretty much control the skies and the air wars, Sietze. It can't be long now."

"I hope not, but it's still plenty dangerous."

Mr. Eilander nodded. "That's for sure. Just last night, many people were murdered in retaliation for the killing of Piet Nobach's son. I know your dad had a run–in with Nobach some time ago, and I was worried about him. Is your dad all right, Sietze?"

With fear–filled eyes, I looked at him and stuttered, "I—I don't really know. Dad left yesterday morning, and he still isn't home."

I had wanted badly to ask Mom where Dad was and when he would be back, but we didn't dare ask questions about those things. We realized that all those details had to remain a secret, and it was possible that even Mom didn't know his hiding place. In the event that Dad lost his life, however, she would surely find out, and we would also know in a hurry—so until then, we kept our curiosity and worry to ourselves. We were assured that Dad was doing everything he possibly could for his own safety and the well–being of his family.

I asked Mr. Eilander, "Do you know any of the people that got killed?"

"*Ja*, Sietze. Don't tell your mom if she doesn't already know it, but her cousin Teake Schuilenga from Surhuisterveen was killed. They found his body this morning along the road in Appelscha."

I stared open–mouthed at Mr. Eilander as he continued.

"The cowards shot him in the back of the head. They murdered Gerrit Beukema right in his own house in front of his family and left him bleeding to death in the hallway. I've heard that several others were murdered, but I haven't heard their names."

I could barely hear Mr. Eilander. The rumble of distant airplanes was thunderous. We both looked up into the sky as it filled with wave upon wave of hundreds of four–engine bombers. Speedy fighter planes surrounded each wave of bombers, keeping the Luftwaffe at bay. Every bomber trailed four vapor trails, which seemed to merge and blend into a giant white cloud. The windows of Mr. Eilander's house rattled, and the earth seemed to vibrate.

We had often seen large Allied bomber fleets with their loads of bombs heading for the heartland of Germany. But never had we seen such huge numbers as were heading toward Germany now.

"Look at that, Sietze," Mr. Eilander yelled over the noise. "They'll be pulverizing Germany. It can't last long now." Still looking at the awesome sight in the sky, he turned and headed back to his house.

What if one of those big bombers accidentally opened its bomb bay doors? I thought.

Formation of B–17's heading for Germany

I lay down on my back in the shade of the Komieze Bos, the small, wooded area where I had once played hide–and–go–seek and war games. I felt safer near the woods as I continued watching the endless armada of bombers heading eastward. The constant droning of a thousand engines dulled my mind, and I drifted into a state of semi–sleep.

Pleasant thoughts of days gone by filled my consciousness, days filled not with fear, but with fun and games and tricks—and some naughtiness. I fondly remembered walking to school every day and sometimes stopping at the little corner store run by an old woman known as Lúts Hiltje. There I would buy one penny's worth of powdered Dutch licorice, which would fill the tip of a small, three–cornered paper bag. If I bought ten cents' worth of candies, Lúts Hiltje would give me a free peppermint. For spending only a nickel, she would bite a peppermint in half with the five remaining teeth in her mouth and hand it to me.

With a jolt, I returned to full alertness. It was very quiet now, with only a few birds chirping in the trees. There wasn't a trace of sound from the heavy aircraft engines. Getting to my feet, I hurried on my way home and wondered if Dad had returned or if Mom had heard about her cousin having been murdered by Piet Nobach and his German executioners

The late summer weather was beautiful, and the sky clear. Even the white clouds of vapor trails had totally dissipated. The sunlight was as comfortable and warm as a satin sheet.

Walking slowly toward home, I felt the unpredictability of our daily lives making room for uneasiness in my mind. I leaned against a large oak tree, trying to concentrate on happy, positive thoughts.

High in the tree above me was a magpie nest, constructed like a fortress of intertwining twigs reinforced with mud. There was only a small opening to allow the birds to enter this little fortress, keeping the growing family safe. Yet at one time, cousin Berend Boersma and I had removed the eggs from the nest nearly every morning. Security was not predictable in the life of a magpie family any more than it was for us.

Arriving home, I found Mom in the kitchen, wrapping up a sandwich and pouring coffee into a thermos bottle. Her eyes were red. I knew she had been crying and must have heard about the murder of her cousin. She was probably still worried about the whereabouts and safety of Dad, too. Mr. Schipper, our refugee in hiding, was nowhere to be seen.

Mom placed the sandwich and thermos bottle in a brown paper bag and turned to me.

"Sietze," she said, "Lewis Smits is in the back field harvesting our field of rye. Will you bring him some lunch?"

"Sure, Mem. I'll do it right away."

"Why don't you take Greta along? She's bored and a little scared."

I took my little sister's hand and headed out the door toward the field of ripened rye, which was the piece of land farthest from the house on our small farm. As we walked along the path, I couldn't help but consider the contrast between the peaceful scenes surrounding us and the possibility of that natural beauty being desecrated by the violence of war.

My little sister stooped to pluck a dandelion flower out of the grass and held it up for me to smell. It hadn't started wilting yet, and even though it was late in the season, I could smell the freshness of the flower and the green fields.

The Way It Was

In the distance, I saw Lewis Smits. He was in perpetual, repetitive motion, cutting down the long stems of rye with a scythe. He would swing the razor–sharp curved blade of the scythe in a forty–five degree arc, moving one step forward after each sweep. Before the end of the day, he would tie the tall rye in bushes and place about ten bundles together upright, forming a teepee–like structure. The formation would help protect the rye from unexpected rain showers and allow for maximum drying prior to threshing.

Greta and I walked between dozens of rye teepees and were only a few feet from Mr. Smits when I heard the sound of an airplane engine. I handed the brown bag to Mr. Smits, and we both looked up.

"You know, Sietze," he said, "that's one of those hundreds of bombers that flew toward Germany a couple of hours ago. This one is coming back all by itself, and you know what that means?"

I shook my head. "No . . . What do you think, Mr. Smits?"

"It looks like there's smoke coming out of the left outboard engine, and I see only two vapor trails. It was probably hit by German anti–aircraft fire and lost two engines. Now it's trying to cripple back to England." Pointing skyward, he added, "Oh goodness, Sietze. This doesn't look good."

B-17 Flying Fortress

I followed the direction his finger was pointing, and then I saw it. Two German fighter planes were sneaking up on the crippled bomber. Each fighter plane was partially hiding in the two vapor trails emanating from the bomber. This tactic would undoubtedly prevent the Flying Fortress tail gunner from seeing the danger that was creeping up on them.

Within moments, we heard the sound of machine guns as the German fighters

Exploding fuel tank separates wing from doomed B-17

commenced their attack. Almost immediately, the B–17 bomb bay doors opened, and we heard the fear–instilling, siren–like whistle of falling bombs. They must have had their entire load of bombs still aboard. Now, in their effort to escape, the bombs had to be jettisoned.

Mr. Smits dropped his lunch bag and headed for the ditch as fast as his bowlegs would carry him. His cap flew off and fell in the field. As the bombs screamed earthward, he picked up speed. I pushed my little sister Greta inside one of the rye teepees and yelled for her to keep her head down on the ground. My heart racing with fear, I lay flat on my back nearby, keeping one hand on Greta's foot while I watched the drama of the dying B–17 unfold. It all happened in seconds, but for me it was like watching a horror show in slow motion.

The German fighters must have hit the left–wing fuel tank. It exploded in a ball of flame, and the entire left wing separated from the Flying Fortress. Bodies began to tumble out of the now fatally stricken machine. Only one parachute opened, and I watched as it lazily floated earthward with a human being swinging like a pendulum below the white nylon canopy. A slight westerly breeze steered the parachute eastward, and I lost sight of it as it neared earth and disappeared behind trees some distance away.

The aircraft's severed wing fluttered through the sky like an aimless airfoil. Spiraling rapidly, the B–17 went into a screaming dive earthward. At the same time, the bombs exploded.

Greta was screaming, and I was scared to death. There was no sign of Lewis Smits. A giant black cloud rose almost straight up from the spot where the Flying Fortress had crashed. From where we were in the back of the rye field, the plane appeared to have crashed slightly beyond our house.

All was quiet again, with no more airplanes in the sky. Only one member of the B–17's crew had escaped a violent death.

Mr. Smits came crawling out of the ditch and picked up his cap on the

Crew of the doomed B-17

way to his lunch bag, which was still lying where he had dropped it. "I think I'll eat my lunch at home, Sietze," he said. With that, he turned and walked across the field toward his home near Topweer.

I pulled Greta out of the rye teepee, and we walked toward home and the rising column of black smoke from the crashed B–17 Flying Fortress.

That evening, Dad returned home safe and sound and in time for dinner. I didn't know where he had gone, and I didn't consider asking. The details were too frightening, and I was just happy to have him back again.

In my wildest dreams, I never could have imagined that almost exactly sixty–two years later, I would learn that the man swinging below that descending parachute was still alive and well.

Another young boy had heard the commotion that day while hiding under his school desk in nearby Surhuisterveen. Frank Weening was nearly twelve years old and did not see the drama of the crashing bomber I had just witnessed. At the instruction of the teacher, he and the rest of his class were lying face–down under their classroom desks. After school, he walked to the site of the smoldering wreckage. As he watched, an open German car approached the crash site. Behind three German soldiers sat a young man in a different uniform, viewing the wreckage sadly. He was clearly a captive of the German soldiers

Even though Frank and I lived only a short distance apart in Holland, we didn't know each other at the time. It would be sixty–two years before Frank contacted me through mutual acquaintances, after learning the identity of the survivor swinging below the billowing parachute. His name was Howard Adams. He was a 23–year–old member of the U.S. Army Air Corps and an engineer and turret gunner aboard the B–17.

Mr. Adams still vividly remembers the day he boarded his Flying Fortress called *Sky Queen* for its final flight:

It was the morning of July 28, 1943. We were awakened at 1:30 a.m. Everyone was sleepy from playing cards the night before. As we came to the mess hall, our officers, who must have gotten up before us, greeted us. Our pilot, Lt. William Dietel, was a tall Texan with an easy–going nature and a reputation for being the top–rated pilot in formation and instrument flying. Our mission briefing would be at 3:30 a.m.

The target was Kassel, Germany, and the final assembly plant of the Focke–Wolfe, Germany's best fighter plane. We were told that our target was heavily defended by German fighters and that we could expect hail-storms of flak coming at us. Fortunately, our Sky Queen was assigned the safest position in our formation. We had always returned safely from our many earlier missions, even when we were assigned more vulnerable formation positions. Surely today would be no different. Or would it? I quickly banished the thought from my mind.

I took my position, together with the other crew members, and the big bomber taxied out and assumed its formation takeoff position. I took my wife's picture from my coverall pocket. For a moment I stared at it lovingly before giving it a last kiss. I always took it with me on missions, knowing that if the Sky Queen went down with her hubby on board, Mrs. Adams would go down with him.

We circled the airport to begin climbing to our assigned altitude and to allow the rest of the formation to join us. Soon the sky was filled with bombers. As the English coastline receded below and behind us, we began scanning the sky for possible hostile aircraft, all the while climbing to 26,000 feet. Various aircraft in our formation experienced a variety of engine and mechanical problems and aborted the mission, returning to the safety of our base in England.

We were over enemy territory now, and the entire crew was on edge. Flak came up at us from multiple ground locations. Some came up in four, six, and eight bursts at a time. The sky was full of it. We test–fired our guns. I waggled my gun up and down to let the other top turret gunners know that all was well. For various reasons, some of the ships were still turning back, and our formation was now less than half its original size. This left us unprotected by other planes from the rear.

The target was now almost in sight, and many German fighters were wait-ing for us. The ball turret gunner called to let us know that several forma-

tions of German fighters were coming up from below. Suddenly I noticed that we were following our lead plane and making a 180-degree turn. We soon learned that our entire formation had been called back to return to base. The mission had been deemed too dangerous. I felt relieved, because our formation was so small now and the German fighters were coming up. I called the navigator and asked him to pass over a German city where I could drop the bombs. He said we were just entering airspace above the Netherlands.

Then the fighters hit us. Their tactic this day was to go for one bomber at a time until they finished him off. I saw several planes go down in smoke behind us, but I never saw anyone bail out. Now we were "tail end Charlie," and I knew we would be next. The fighters hit us like a pack of vultures. I could feel the vibrations of the ship from the pounding of our own machine guns. The ball turret gunner came up and reported that our number two engine had a hole in its cowling and was smoking. From my position, I couldn't see the hole, but I could see the trail of smoke.

I saw a Focke-Wolfe attempt a head-on attack. He was high enough that I could get him in my sights, and I let him have a long burst, never letting up on the triggers. His plane fell over on its right wing. His prop almost seemed to stop. Flames and smoke poured out from all over the front half of his fighter, and I knew that I had gotten him.

Suddenly, above the noise of rushing air in my turret, I heard the sound of bullets ripping through the airplane, then an enormously loud "whoom" as though a large shell had burst right in front of me. The aircraft nosed over and went into a screaming dive. Immediately I saw that Lt. Dietel had been killed and was lying over the controls.

I hit the interphone button and told the crew to bail out. Then I jerked the emergency handle at the edge of the bomb bay, opening the doors and releasing the bombs. G-forces nearly pinned me to the spot, and moving required great effort. I managed to snap on my chute, stepped into the bomb bay, and reached for the ripcord so I would have a hold of it when I hit the air. It was then that I realized my parachute pack was upside down. No time to change. I grabbed the ripcord with my left hand and bailed out.

Prey and Predators

The instant force of the slipstream must have pulled my left arm holding the ripcord. My parachute opened immediately with a tremendous jerk. I had enough presence of mind to put my oxygen tube in my mouth, and my mental acuity quickly returned to normal. The scene had changed from a roaring hell to a deathly stillness. A helpless, sickly feeling seized me. Would enemy fighters come and strafe me? I had heard that this was not uncommon.

As the ground neared, I braced myself for the landing. I impacted pastureland with spine–jarring force. It was very painful, and I didn't feel able to move from my prone position. But I had to try to get away. I threw my collapsed chute into a ditch.

In no time, Dutch citizens surrounded me. Someone explained that a Nazi sympathizer had notified the authorities and I wouldn't be able to escape. I was given hot coffee and hot milk with several sandwiches. In return, I didn't resist parting with my helmet, goggles, squadron emblem, and even my flying boots. Due to my spine injury, I was barely able to walk. The local doctor who looked me over explained in broken English that I had no broken bones.

Soon, three German soldiers arrested me. They put me in the back of an open car and drove me to the crash site of what had been my airplane. The once proud Sky Queen was still smoldering. The tail of the plane was standing upright in another field, and one of the engines lay in another field. That was where my German captors took me.

I was asked to identify a body. The top of the head had been blown away, and a feeling of sickness crept over me. The face was swollen beyond recognition. When the body was turned over, I saw the nameplate on the jacket: Jack L. Mason. He was our tail gunner. His body had been thrown clear when the tail broke off from the fuselage. Except for one other survivor, radio operator Perrotti, this was the place where the lives of my crew members had abruptly ended.

My captors soon made it clear that for me, the war was over. I was taken to a hospital in Leeuwarden, where I stayed for five days before being transferred to Dijlag–Luft in Frankfurt, Germany. After being interrogated, I was moved to POW camp Stalag 7A, near Munich.

The Way It Was

Thus ended the eighth and final mission of the Sky Queen *and her crew. May my fellow crew members, who died for world peace and freedom, rest in peace.*

The crew of the perished B-17 were buried in Opende in 1943. Pictured of flight crew memorial in Opende cemetery.

T Sgt. Howard Adams Survivor of the final flight of the B-17 "Flying Fortress."

 # A FINAL RECKONING

I walked home on the evening of May 4, 1945, after visiting with my friend Jan Westra.

Everywhere, conversation revolved around the end of the war. Hitler had committed suicide in his bunker in Berlin. The southern parts of Holland had already been liberated. Thousands of Dutch underground resistance workers were now coming above–ground, dressed in blue coveralls and wearing orange bands around their left arms. Joining the Canadian liberation forces, they were eliminating the last pockets of German military contingencies still able to put up a fight. They also rounded up and arrested the traitors and Dutch Nazi sympathizers who had collaborated with the Germans during the past five years.

The sun was long down, but somehow it didn't seem to want to get dark. The evening was unusually warm for spring. All over the neighborhood, small groups of people were talking. Children were up and playing in the twilight. Some homes had lights shining brightly through the windows, indicating that the citizens were already beginning to disregard the German wartime rules. In the distance could be heard the alternately mournful and joyful chirps of birds preparing to protect their nests during the approaching night. It was as if all of nature held its collective breath in preparation for the liberation.

Sleep eluded me for hours. I had hoped and prayed that I would live to be at least eighteen years old so I could serve in the resistance, but I knew now that I wouldn't have survived long as a double agent. The idea had occupied my planning for the past five years; now we were hearing that this awful war would be over soon.

Could I actually start thinking about a real future, about a girlfriend, a wife, a family, a career? No, that still seemed too unreal.

I punched my head into the pillow and finally drifted into dreamland.

Dad woke me up at six o'clock the next morning. It was milking time and a beautiful day. I was reminded of that May morning five years earlier.

"Good morning, Sietze," Dad said. He smiled and seemed in an uncharacteristically good mood.

"Morning, Dad," I responded.

We heard a truck racing along the street a short distance away. Dad stood up from his milk stool to get a better look, and I did the same.

"Those are not German soldiers, Sietze," he said. "They're Dutch resistance freedom fighters. They're chasing the remnants of German resistance and arresting German sympathizer NSB–ers." NSB stood for the National Socialistic *Beweging*, or the National Socialist Movement.

"You think they're going to arrest Piet Nobach, and maybe his brother Folkert?" I asked.

Dad nodded. "I think they'll nab them if they can find the cowards." Almost jubilantly, he added, "I think the war will be over before the day is over."

"This could be an exciting day, Dad."

"I think so, Sietze, but it could still be dangerous out in the streets. You and Henk better be very careful."

I was elated. Clearly Dad had not given me any work assignments for the day.

"Hey, Dad, can I have that old radio I buried? I don't think it'll work anymore, anyway."

"So you did bury our old radio?" Dad asked.

"Yes, I did, and I still can't tell you where I buried it. If it's safe now, I'd like to dig it up, and maybe the pistol, too."

"It may be safe today, Sietze, but you'd better wait until tomorrow. Then we'll know if and how the liberation unfolds."

Brother Henk was sitting on the wooden gate, looking toward the road.

"Look, Sietze," he said. "A few small trucks and cars are speeding along the street. I don't think they're German vehicles. I've seen at least two trucks with men in blue coveralls and an orange armband standing in the back with guns. One even had a machine gun mounted on the roof of the truck cab. What's happening?"

I looked across the small field toward the street and said, "Dad thinks that today will be the liberation of the northern provinces of Groningen and Friesland. Those men in blue coveralls are no longer underground resistance fighters. They've openly joined the Canadian liberation forces to help them mop up remnants of German strongholds, and they're arresting the Dutch traitors who helped the Germans during the past five years."

"Let's walk to the center of town, Sietze. Maybe they'll capture Folkert Nobach."

"And I hope they catch Piet Nobach, too," I said. "He was a lot worse than his brother Folkert. Dad said it could still be dangerous on the street today. If the freedom fighters encounter German soldiers, there will be a gunfight."

"*Ja*, we'd better be pretty careful. Let's walk behind the big oak trees. If we see or hear something dangerous, we can drop in the dry ditch along the road."

We climbed the wooden gate and headed out across the pasture.

Cautiously we walked along the shoulder of the road, near the ditch that ran behind the line of oak trees. A man who was clearly in a rush pedaled his bicycle toward Opende and didn't seem to notice us.

Near the Van der Veen home, we noticed a small group of people, including some children, all in animated conversation. We cautiously crossed the street toward the assembled group. Henk Boersma, my brother's friend and schoolmate, was also heading for the road. Henk quickly joined his buddy, and together we mingled with the Van der Veen family and other neighbors.

"Has anybody seen Folkert Nobach or his son Bertus today?" somebody asked.

Hielko Lettinga piped up. "I saw a fellow in a black uniform go to the Nobach home this morning."

"I'll bet they know that this is likely to be D–Day for them," another man said.

A truck came roaring along, heading in the direction of Surhuisterveen. A machine gun was mounted on the cab, and there were about a dozen heavily armed Dutch freedom fighters on the bed of the truck. It slowed down slightly as it approached our group.

One of the soldiers yelled, "We're hunting for Piet Nobach, and we'll get the bastard!"

The group shouted and clapped as the truck sped off.

I wandered off in the direction of the center of town. Henk and his friend were already ahead of me, walking in the same direction. Finding that group of people must have emboldened them, because they were not even using the oak trees as cover. I saw Dad's bicycle parked against the side of the Folkerts' home and clothing shop.

I grinned as I walked past Wijma's Café. Memories came to mind of drunken old Bouke Peuter's bicycle resting against the wall with a plug of chewing tobacco on the saddle awaiting his return. I wanted to start laughing uproariously but decided I had better look around to make sure no one else was within earshot, lest I be branded an idiot.

In the distance, I noticed a speeding truck approaching from the direction of Surhuisterveen. From where I was standing, it looked like a military vehicle, with machine guns mounted on the cab. I froze, afraid for a moment that the truck was German. The nearest oak tree was nearly 300 yards away, and there wasn't enough time to make a run for it. I felt like a deer caught in the bright beam of a poacher's searchlight.

Not daring to look, I was startled by the sound of screeching brakes. With profound relief, I saw that the truck was loaded with heavily armed Dutch freedom fighters, members of the *Nederlandse Binnenlandse Strijdkrachten*, or NBS.

Farm house where Mr. and Mrs. Nobach lived

The truck came to a screeching halt directly in front of the Nobach farmhouse. Soldiers jumped from the truck and, with weapons at the ready, carefully approached the house.

Within moments, shots were fired through the windows from inside. All the soldiers immediately dropped to the ground and commenced returning fire into the house through the already shattered windows. I quickly hid behind a large oak tree directly across the street from the Nobach home.

Clearly this would not be a peaceful surrender, and I now found myself virtually in the middle of a battle. Lethal bullets were flying, and I was scared even behind the big tree.

Sagging to my knees to further minimize my exposure, I carefully peeked around the tree trunk. Just then, I saw Nobach's son Bertus, probably in his late twenties, coming out of the side door with his arms and hands high in the air, waving a white handkerchief as a sign of surrender. He seemed to be wounded on the forehead, perhaps by flying glass from the shattered windows.

Two soldiers covered his wound with a white cloth and bound his wrists. Then they took him away from the battle area and guarded him at the street. Some people taunted him, and a few slapped him.

The small decorative window in the front door of the Nobach home was also shot out. One soldier was crawling on his stomach toward the front door. As he reached it, he took a hand grenade from his belt and removed the safety pin. He quickly tossed the grenade through the small, broken front door window. He didn't notice that the door was beginning to open just as he hurled the grenade.

There was a terrific explosion. Then, suddenly, it was quiet—no more gunfire into the house, and no response fire from within the house. Carefully the soldiers inched toward the house with guns pointed toward every shattered window, nervously looking for movement.

Two shots were fired from seemingly deep within the house. It sounded like two guns had been fired almost simultaneously. Several tense minutes elapsed before the first soldiers tentatively entered the house. The gathered crowds seemed to hold their collective breath. Another few minutes passed before the front door opened and two soldiers emerged, carrying what appeared to be a quickly fashioned stretcher that bore a blanket–covered body.

Deserting my hiding place behind the big oak tree, I walked across the street. Two soldiers carried the body right past me. The head was covered, but the hands, dress, and feet were visible. I knew it was Folkert Nobach's wife. Since her body had been found right behind the front door, it was later assumed that she had just started opening the door in surrender when the grenade was thrown through the shattered window, killing her instantly. Two more soldiers exited the house through the side door, carrying a body on a primitive stretcher, followed by one more body with its head covered.

The crowd of townspeople and neighbors grew silent now. Some had gleeful expressions on their faces. Somehow, in the presence of death—even the deaths of enemies—their expressions seemed out of place to me. The bodies were carried about one block to the small town hall across from the *Gereformeerde* church where I had been baptized. Even the Nobachs had been long–time members there.

Most of the townspeople began dispersing and heading home. Only a few entered the small town hall, where the bodies were laid on long tables. There was hushed conversation.

I overheard one man say that Nobach and his uniformed compatriot had shot each other in the temple on command. That would explain the two shots occurring almost simultaneously. It could have been speculation, but someone also may have been looking through one of the small windows in the rear of the farmhouse.

I stood next to the body of Folkert Nobach. His head was covered with a blanket, and he was still wearing one wooden shoe. I jumped when I saw his feet move and twitch. I half–expected him to remove the blanket from his head and say, "Hi, Sietze boy. How are you?"

The booted feet of the uniformed man were not moving, nor were Mrs. Nobach's feet.

Suddenly, looking around, I realized I was the only one left in the small hall. I felt scared; I was alone among the dead. Quietly, I slipped through the door and began slowly walking toward home.

My solemn introspection was interrupted by the sound of a truck coming from the direction of Surhuisterveen. I paused to watch. Remaining spectators along the street began yelling in jubilation.

Then I saw him. Piet Nobach had been captured alive and was now tied firmly to the front bumper and radiator grille of the vehicle. He had an

understandably tortured expression on his face. There was no doubt that he was quite uncomfortable. He could not have known yet that his brother and family had just died.

I crossed to the other side of the street, away from the groups of people. I wanted to be alone. A gentle breeze whooshed through the emerg-

Piet Nobach tied to the front of a truck being captured

ing leaves on the large oak trees, casting golden reflections from an already setting sun.

I tried to make sense of what I had just witnessed: the death of Mr. Nobach, the man who for the past five years had regarded me as his friend. He had even believed me when I had lied to him about the identity of the lady he had seen by the clothesline. Yet he had caused me to fear for the life of my family. Had he not believed me, my whole family might have been killed. Now I would never have to suffer such life–threatening worries again. Why wasn't I glad that he was dead now? Why did I feel so sad?

Because of the German occupation and the corroboration of traitors like Mr. Nobach, I had feared for my life and expected instant death on more than one occasion. Now Mr. Nobach had looked death squarely in the face. I knew what that felt like. He must have known that for him, it was inevitable, inescapable, final—bang, and you're dead! Thousands of patriotic, heroic resistance fighters had faced a German firing squad with the same inevitability, often because of the traitorous actions of people like the Nobachs.

Yes, his brother Piet certainly deserved to die. The blood of many of his patriotic countrymen was on his hands. But Folkert Nobach was not nearly that bad. To me, he was basically a peaceful man, as were his wife and son Bertus.

Then a thought struck me. Mom had told me that Dad had had a dangerous run-in with Piet Nobach one day. Piet had told him that he planned to be in church on Sunday and partake of communion. Dad replied that the elders had decided that Nobach would not be allowed to partake of communion, and Piet had promised he would get even. But his brother Folkert liked me. Could he have told his brother to leave our family alone? He certainly knew that the boy he liked would have been very sad if his dad were killed.

I lay down in the berm behind the oak trees, feeling as if I were floating in a sea of mixed emotions. I would never get answers to my questions.

The magpies were busy building their nest, preparing to raise their offspring in peace and without fear. I vowed that I would never again remove the eggs from a magpie nest.

Completely alone now, I walked home. I went behind the pig and horse barn to the small building where the potatoes were cooked for consumption by our pigs. No one could see me here. I had fallen to my knees on this very same spot as a naïve ten-year-old, filled with uncertainty and fear. I had asked God to keep our whole family and me safe.

Almost five years had passed since that day. Now it was time to thank God for answering that prayer and the hundreds of others I had prayed during the intervening years.

The war was over. It was May 5, 1945.

# TOWARD NEW BEGINNINGS

The days of crashing airplanes, violent aerial dogfights, screaming bombs, and flying bullets were over now. It took me a while to fully understand that these events would linger forever in my mind as vivid memories of that fearful five–year war. We enjoyed peace and freedom once again.

The urge to explore new realities, possibilities, and horizons, which for so long had been impossible to contemplate, began to arouse a young man's curiosity. Often, a cavalcade of images and ideas about a future I had not dared dream of for so long came to me in the peaceful, secret retreat of my imagination.

Soon after the death of Folkert Nobach, Mr. Schipper and his family returned to their hometown of Heerenveen, which was now safe and free of the Germans. Before departing, he presented us with a little plaque as an expression of gratitude. The plaque hung on the wall for a long time. After that we never saw or heard from him again, to the deep disappointment of my parents, who had demonstrated that they were truly willing to give their lives to help Mr. Schipper. They spoke of him frequently, wondering what had become of him.

Mom did receive a letter from her two cousins in America. They lived in Lynden, Washington, and were no doubt wondering if their cousin Aafke and her family had survived the war. Thus began a period of regular correspondence between Mom and her cousins. Frequently, there were long and what seemed like secretive conversations between Mom and Dad.

Early one evening, Mom said, "Sietze, what do you think about emigrating to America?"

Even though I had recently read a headline in the provincial newspaper, which called America "the land of unlimited opportunities," I wasn't at all excited about the idea. I had begun dabbling in electronics and had started a little business called Radio Veenron with my friend Klaas Veenstra. On Sunday evenings, another friend, Jan Westra, and I would go searching far and wide for a girlfriend.

I was also in regular correspondence with a girl named Ali Heyboer, whom I had met at a church–related youth convention in Groningen. I had not seen her since the convention because she lived in Rotterdam, South Holland, while I lived in the province of Friesland at the other end of the country.

Life was good. Why would I want to move thousands of miles away, where I didn't know anybody and didn't even know the language? I would probably have to work on a farm, and I wasn't interested in becoming a farmer. Dad probably thought that someday I would come to my senses.

"We think that emigrating might be best for our children's futures," Mom was saying. "But if you and Henk aren't interested, we might drop the idea."

I could tell that she and Dad would be disappointed. I couldn't understand why they would want to emigrate, since they had their small farm paid for. There was a hired man, and Dad was already a little over fifty. I said I would think about it.

Late one winter evening in early 1948, I walked across the field that had once belonged to the late Folkert Nobach, toward the house where my Boersma cousins had once lived. It had been converted into a tavern. As I walked in through the front door, the owner, Mr. Boonstra, asked what I wanted.

"Just lemonade, Mr. Boonstra," I responded as I seated myself on a wooden chair.

I was the only client in the place. Mr. Boonstra brought the good–tasting greenish liquid and sat down to chat.

"I hear your parents are thinking of emigrating to America, Sietze. Is that true?"

"*Ja*, that's true, but I'm not at all excited about it, so it may not happen. That's just fine with me."

"What?" he said with incredulity. "You're not excited about it? You're crazy!"

"Why?"

"Because you're a young man. It's an enormous adventure, and you can always come back and start your life here if you don't like it. But your dad is over fifty. Why would he start all over again in a strange country?"

I hadn't thought of it as an adventure for me, but it made a lot of sense. Perhaps I should change my mind and tell Mom and Dad that I was enthused about the family emigration plans.

"Mr. Boonstra, if you think my parents are crazy for wanting to emigrate at their age, why would they be thinking of doing it?"

"Sietze, I don't know your parents too well. But, you know, I get a good number of townspeople in here. They order a beer or a Beerenburg, and they want to talk."

"Do some people talk about my folks' plans to emigrate?"

"*Ja*, sure, Sietze. Everybody is talking about it in Opende."

I was surprised. "Do they have any idea why my folks want to go to America?"

"Well, you know, your dad is quite a prominent man in town." I had never thought of Dad as being a prominent man in Opende. "He was the band director of Crescendo for many years, a church elder, a school board member, a successful farmer and business man. Not many people from these parts are emigrating. Besides, most are going to Canada, and most are poor farm labor people who would like to make their lives better. Your parents don't fit that category at all."

I looked at Mr. Boonstra in rapt attention and was quiet for a while.

"No, Mr. Boonstra, I don't think of my folks as poor. And that's precisely why it's hard to understand them wanting to leave the achievements of their life behind. Is that what you're saying?"

"That's right, Sietze, and my regulars can't figure it out, either. But they all have their theories."

"Can you tell me some of the theories?" I asked. I had always viewed my parents in a certain light, which I now realized might be completely different from the way other grownups in the town viewed them.

Dad (centered front) founded the now famous band "Crescendo" in 1922

"Well, you know that during the war, your folks were with the resistance movement. Some think it has a lot to do with the fact that after the war, the former Nazi sympathizers merely got a slap on the wrist. After a few weeks in jail, they were sent back to their homes again. Even the treacherous Piet Nobach got off practically scot–free. I understand that he lives in The Hague and runs a small tavern.

Crescendo in 2006 is now a world famous bicycle show band.

That kind of injustice doesn't sit well with your folks, who were prepared to give their lives to save a countryman. There's Piet Nobach with the blood of many of his countrymen on his hands, sitting fat and sassy in business in The Hague."

Yes, I had often overheard snatches of conversation between my parents expressing anger with the Dutch government for coddling the formerly feared traitors. I wondered how many other people in the town knew that my parents had been active in the underground movement. Mr. Boonstra obviously did.

For a moment I stared at the floor in deep thought, forgetting to sip my lemonade. Then I lifted my head and nodded my understanding. Mr. Boonstra could tell I wanted to hear more "theories."

"Sietze, maybe you don't know, but I am not a church–going man. I hear some of my regulars talk about a split in your church. You know, of course, that your dad and Dominee Van Dijk led a small group of people who protested some new teachings of the *Gereformeerde* church."

"Sure," I said. "I even helped when they were building the new church next to barber Kuperus's home."

Led by my father, the group had started meeting in a large café room and later built a small church named the *Gereformeerde Vrijgemaakte Kerk*, or Christian Reformed Liberated church.

Although the doctrines of the new church didn't vary too much from the original church, some people had decided that they didn't agree sufficiently to remain one denomination. I remembered frequent debates about religion during the war years, revolving around intricate doctrinal differences that ultimately split the church. I never got very excited about the issues, feeling that the animosity they created was not consistent with what I believe to be the first and greatest commandment in Christian faith. That principle seemed to go out the window when the church members debated issues like predestination and presumed regeneration.

Mr. Boonstra poured some more lemonade in my glass, which was still more than half full. He sat down at the small, round bar table directly across from me.

"I don't have any cows, pigs, or chickens," he said, "so I don't need to buy any farm animal feed. But I understand that your dad lost a lot of good clients who used to buy all their feed and fertilizer from him. I heard that was because he helped spearhead the small group of people who split from your church, and many didn't agree with him."

Mr. Boonstra clearly knew a lot of things a boy of nearly eighteen years rarely thought about. He was right. I knew I wasn't delivering nearly as much dairy grain as the year before. I was beginning to see some of the reasons that made leaving Opende appealing to my parents.

"Another thing the locals often talk about," Boonstra added, "is a widespread fear that the communists are soon going to rule all of Europe, including Holland."

It was another subject I had heard my parents talk about, so I listened attentively as he continued.

"*Ja*, I even worry about that myself sometimes. I can tell you this, Sietze—if those damned communists take over this country, it's going to be a lot worse than it was under the Germans."

I could tell he was not a church–going man. And I could understand that, after surviving the perils of World War II, Mom and Dad wouldn't be very eager to expose the family to new dangers. Besides, our family had now grown to include my little sister Mary. Born in 1946, she was a little less than two years old now and the little darling of the family.

Mr. Boonstra removed his cap and vigorously scratched his bald head before covering it with the cap again and looking at me.

"Then, Sietze, there are a few people who think that your dad never got over his disappointment when the brass band Crescendo decided to get another director. I don't think your dad ever got paid for all those years that he organized and directed it. Not that he expected that, or would have even accepted it. It was his hobby. He was good at music, and he loved it. Some think that he's still bitter about being rejected as director. They wanted him to stay in the band, but he never wanted anything to do with it after that."

I hadn't noticed the front door of the little tavern open until the loud bell rang. I looked through the window at the now dark sky as Mr. Boonstra got busy with his new client. I took one more sip from the still unfinished glass of lemonade, wished Mr. Boonstra a good night, and slipped out the front door.

I wandered across the field very slowly. Occasionally the moon would attempt to pierce the racing, wind–driven clouds. I had so much to think about. Being a curious person, I was curious about America. This suddenly seemed like an enormously attractive opportunity. As Mr. Boonstra had pointed out to me, I was young and could come back if I chose.

Yes, I had made up my mind. Even though I had trouble with the thought of leaving everything behind, I would tell my parents that I was all in favor of emigrating to America.

———————

Toward New Beginnings

It was the evening of May 20, 1948. Our house was full of company. Many of our uncles and aunts were there, and some of our closest family friends, too.

We all had mixed feelings about the departure. It was a somber gathering, much like a wake, with many farewells being exchanged. There seemed to be a cloud of sadness that hovered above those who were leaving and those who would be left behind.

Many people of that age had not yet fully realized that the world was beginning to shrink, in a sense. Because of the still–evolving airline transportation industry, departing loved ones didn't really have to view such departures as final farewells . . . but most people didn't know that then. People in those days couldn't imagine going back and forth over oceans. The only way to go was by ship, and the journey from one continent to another over the Atlantic Ocean would take about ten days. Since air travel was in its infancy, there were apparently no flights at that time between the American continent and the European continent. The sense of a final farewell permeated the gathering in our house that evening.

My mother's brother, Uncle Marten Hoekstra, had a taxi and bus transportation business in Veenwouden. He would be picking us up at three o'clock in the morning to take the family to the Rotterdam harbor. People came and went all evening, with much handshaking and solemn farewells. I visited with Jan Westra. He would accompany me on the bus for the long trip from Opende to Rotterdam.

It was pitch dark when more than thirty people walked across the pastureland to the waiting bus. Mom and Dad looked back one more time. The place where their married life had begun, where they had raised their family, where they had experienced the joys and fears of life in every dimension, was merely a dark silhouette now. I'm not sure if Dad waved a feeble salute to the place he was forever leaving behind. He may have had a premonition that he would never see it again.

We spent the final day of our life in the Netherlands in Rotterdam. We arrived early in the morning, although the ship didn't leave until four o'clock in the afternoon. We spent our remaining time with the relatives and friends who had accompanied us to the dock before quietly—almost reluctantly—boarding the *MS Veendam* headed for America.

Slowly the ship began moving along the Maas River on its way to the North Sea. It was just our family now. Leaning over the railing on one of the top decks of the ship, we waved our last farewells to all the loved ones ashore.

Even as the figures of our family and friends grew too small to recognize, there was one figure I could still discern. It was my Rotterdam girlfriend, Ali Heyboer. She was walking along the shore of the wide river, waving a white handkerchief. Seeing her waiting at the dock, I realized that her feelings might have been stronger than mine. I watched her and waved until she, too, faded from view. We would never see each other again.

 **AFTERWORD**

My family's voyage to America lasted about eleven days. My mother was seasick the entire time, a situation that was not improved by the stormy weather.

Feeling a strong sense that adventure awaited me, I stood at the railing on the top deck of the ship as the awesome sight of the Statue of Liberty came into view. The train ride that followed our voyage at sea lasted five days. While passing through the Chicago area, I saw my first stretch limousine. I had never seen a long car like that before in my life, and my eyes were surely bugging out in awe.

I never knew one way or the other how strongly my Rotterdam girl-friend Ali Heyboer may have felt for me. We corresponded for a short time after my arrival in America, but not for long. I was in my new country for only a week or two before I met my wife to be, Margaret.

Why my parents decided to move to America is a question that has been the source of many hours of conversation between myself and my brother Henry.

Our best insight into the mystery came to us during a visit that Hank and I made to Holland with our wives. An aging aunt in Friesland—my mother's sister – told us that a number of reasons had come together to persuade them, in much the same way Mr. Boonstra had described.

The most influential reasons, my aunt suggested, were Mom and Dad's enormous disappointment with the way the traitors were dealt with after the liberation; the nasty split in the church, which cost my Dad many dairy feed customers; and the real fear of Russian communism overwhelming Europe.

Interestingly, Dad may have had a change of heart regarding the issues that split the church, because in America he was propositioned by a small church of exactly the same doctrinal standards as the one he had split from. He joined the American Christian Reformed Church and remained there for the next five years of his life, until he suddenly fell ill. Due to insufficient medical care at that time, he passed away within only twenty–four hours.

I often asked my mother about the move to America, but she always remained mum on the subject. Perhaps she regretted the decision. Those first few years were indeed a cruel paradise for so many immigrants to this country.

Of course, the truth about Hitler's concentration camps and the roundup of the Jews came to light soon after the liberation. Abe, the Jewish cattle dealer, had been right when he said that Hitler's plan for the Netherlands included the gradual elimination of Dutch Jews.

Very few of the hundreds of thousands of Jews in Holland survived the war. The last train to leave a concentration camp in Holland headed for Auschwitz in September of 1944. That train was carrying Anne Frank, the famous teenager who was in hiding with her Jewish family in a now famous house in Amsterdam, which has since become known as the Anne Frank House. She was transported from a concentration camp in Holland to a concentration camp in Germany, from which she never returned.

*Howard Adams, the parachuting survivor of the crashed Flying Fortress, never forgot his fallen comrades. After nearly two years of solitary confinement in prisoner–of–war camps in Germany, he returned to his wife and home in the U.S. Every year on the twenty–eighth day of July, he raises the flag at half–staff in memory of his *Sky Queen* crewmates who perished on their final mission. All of them had developed strong bonds of friendship and mutual respect.

There was Shorty Dunmeyer, the ball turret gunner. He was small and looked like an eighteen–year–old, but at twenty–seven, Shorty was the oldest of the crew. He was liked by all the crew members. Ed Amory, the assistant engineer, was a dark boy from New York. He was a good–natured young man who had operated a sporting goods store before his Army career. The pilot, Lt. William Dietel, was a tall, handsome Texan with a helpful, easy–going nature. He had married shortly before his overseas assignment.

Lt. Davis was the bombardier. He was a chubby young man with a jolly disposition. Ardell Bollinger was the radio operator for the *Sky Queen*, but because of an ear infection, he was replaced by Perrotti, the B–17's one other survivor. Jack Mason was the tail gunner. If the crew needed transportation to or from the aircraft before or after missions, Jack never had a problem "appropriating" the nearest vehicle in sight. His nickname was Motor Pool Mason.

The images and memories of those comrades have flashed through Howard Adams' mind a million times. All were young men whose lives ended abruptly in July 1943.

During a visit to the Netherlands, Adams walked silently amidst the sea of white marble crosses at the American Military Cemetery in Margraten, where his fallen comrades were reinterred after being moved from a cemetery in Opende. Standing on the crest of a hill, he was overcome with emotions as he saw the thousands of crosses standing like silent sentinels on that beautiful spring day. Here, in a quiet cemetery, rested the mortal remains of those who would never see the tomorrows they fought for — the young who died before their time, leaving a legacy of dreams that would never materialize. Here lay his fallen crew members, their lives and talents lost forever. They would never see another dawn or watch another sunset, never again feel the warm embrace of their loved ones. May the world never forget.

The Way It Was

Returning to the entrance, Adams paused to read the memorial inscribed in the marble wall:

O Lord support us all the day long
Until the shadows lengthen and the evening comes
And the fever of life is over and our work is done
Then in thy mercy grant us a safe lodging, a holy rest
And peace at the last.

 **POSTSCRIPT**

The reader may have noticed that the five–year period between 1940 and 1945 fills far more pages of memories than the first ten years of my life. The reasons, I believe, are two–fold. First, the years between the ages of ten and fifteen are probably the most formative years of a human life. Second, the events of World War II not only molded and impacted my life, but also shaped the world during the second half of the twentieth century. I developed a lifelong interest in the details of the war and have devoted a great deal of time to researching the first few days of the German invasion of the Netherlands. Those terrifying events affected me deeply and impacted my life, perhaps even shaping my personality to some degree.

The war years forever burned into my being the values my parents taught us, not in the classroom of routine daily living, but through their actions in the midst of the firestorm of life. My parents knew the risks of execution if they were discovered hiding a fellow human being. They demonstrated through example that the first and greatest commandments—to love God and love your fellow man – were principles that they would never compromise, even in the face of death. They demonstrated their unyielding commitment to the values of loyalty and patriotism. For the rest of my life, I will appreciate the values they taught me and admire the strength of character they demonstrated during their journey.

Finally, I have stood among the thousands of white marble crosses in the American Military Cemetery in Margraten, the Netherlands. Tears trickled down my cheeks as I read the name on a marker and thought about the sacrifice of that young individual and countless other young men who gave their lives. Captain Roger Perkins and a million like him gave his life, allowing me to enjoy freedom and peace and to raise a family of children, grandchildren, and great–grandchildren.

I owe these soldiers a debt of gratitude I can never repay. But I will forever honor the memory of those who sacrificed their lives, as well as those who, like my parents, so valiantly resisted the oppressive yoke of Hitler's Nazi occupation of the Netherlands during the years 1940–1945.

Sid Baron

 # ABOUT THE AUTHOR

The author was born in the Netherlands and emigrated with his family after the Second World War. He has enjoyed a successful entrepreneurial career in starting a variety of businesses, including a commercial FM broadcast station, electronic and telecommunication companies, a construction and development company, and several others. He is still actively involved in ownership and management of a large construction company, a few small hotels, and other facilities. He frequently speaks at public meetings or events and has held leadership positions in various civic, church, and charitable organizations. Spending time with the families of any or all of his six children is always a blessed pleasure, as well as flying his airplane for business and pleasure.

The author loves to hear from readers and personally responds to all mail and e–mail.